Daniel Worcester Faunce

Inspiration Considered as a Trend

Daniel Worcester Faunce

Inspiration Considered as a Trend

ISBN/EAN: 9783337183271

Printed in Europe, USA, Canada, Australia, Japan

Cover: Foto ©ninafisch / pixelio.de

More available books at **www.hansebooks.com**

INSPIRATION
CONSIDERED AS A TREND

BY
D. W. FAUNCE, D. D.
Author of "Hours with a Sceptic"

PHILADELPHIA
AMERICAN BAPTIST PUBLICATION SOCIETY
1896

Copyright 1896 by the
AMERICAN BAPTIST PUPLICATION SOCIETY

From the Society's own Press

Dedicated
TO
Rev. W. H. P. FAUNCE, D. D.
MY SON IN THE FLESH
IN THE SPIRIT
AND IN THE MINISTRY OF THE GOSPEL

PREFATORY NOTE

In his former volume entitled, "Prayer as a Theory and a Fact," the "Fletcher Prize Essay," the author of this book attempted to show that prayer involves two persons, God and man. The various lines of proof for the Divine existence were briefly named. They all show direction rather than attainment. It was said, "These various ways of seizing upon the idea of God are by no means exclusive of each other. They are methods suited to unlike minds. But there are minds so constituted that an unmistakable *trend* is more convincing than the sight of the ultimate goal. Enclosed in a circular box that men call a compass, is a delicate needle which, however you disturb it, trembles back to its pole. And it does this because all over the earth run unseen magnetic currents converging toward an unseen magnetic center far away in the north. Men sail on every ocean of the world and measure their land on every continent of the globe by that trend of the magnetic currents toward the pole. But no mortal foot ever touched that pole, no mortal eye ever saw it. It is the world over only a trend. And not only the earth beneath, but the wide heavens above us, are mapped off in lines of gigantic boundary by the steady trend toward a pole no man ever saw or touched.

The trend toward God in all forms of human thought is just as distinct."

This volume aims to carry out and newly apply the thought of trend as there expressed. The form of argument used there for the Divine existence is used here for the Divine inspiration. It is insisted that trend, the strongest proof in the one case, is the strongest proof in the other. What if the method God intended us to use in proving his own being and his own revelation is one? So too, it may be that the trend in the various theories of inspiration proposed by devout students of the Bible and that shown by the Bible itself, deserve notice. No new theory is here proposed; but the theories devoutly held and the facts declared and involved in the Scriptures and confirmed in the Christian experience, are passed in brief review—to find in them all an unmistakable trend.

So broad a subject as this of inspiration will present itself to men under various aspects. It can be studied in manifold relations. It may be considered as an inbreathing with reference to its source, or as an impulse with reference to its power. It may be considered as a process with reference to its method, or as a product with reference to its results as found in a book. Only one of the many ways of considering the subject is here undertaken—that of *trend*. Hence the title, " Inspiration Considered as a Trend."

It is to be remembered that "trend," like all our mental and moral terms, was primarily used in a physical sense. It is now used to signify the tendency that makes for an end and also for the potency that gains it. The "magnetic trend" in physics is a term employed not only to describe a tendency, but to define a force attaining constantly a definite end. Used in political, in literary, in historical, and in moral statement, it declares not only developmental direction, but achieved potency covering alike process and result.

Nor let any man think that the idea of trend reduces inspiration to its lowest terms. Trends do indeed differ in intensity. But the accumulation of facts which show the potency of this trend, raises the certainty and the character of this method of proof above that of any one theory or of all theories, and so lifts it into the highest possible position.

If the satisfaction gained by a fresh study of this view of inspiration shall equal, in the mind of any reader, that enjoyed by the writer of these pages in their preparation, he will be abundantly rewarded.

D. W. F.

Pawtucket, R. I.

CONTENTS

CHAPTER I

THE SUBJECT STATED

SECTION I. THE QUESTIONS INVOLVED, ... 13
Importance of the subject. Duty of investigation and decision. The burden of proof. The men who accept the Book as inspired. The interests at stake. Definiteness or indefiniteness of belief and conviction. The "burning question."

SECTION II. THE RECOGNITION OF TREND, ... 30
Differing theories. Each may help. No one of them held in absolute consistency. All show a trend. The trend the chief thing. The methods to be used in seeking the trend.

CHAPTER II

THE GATHERED MATERIAL

SECTION I. OUR NATURAL INTUITIONS, ... 42
Limitations of the inductive method. New Testament basis may be questioned. Old Testament also. Going back to our "original intuitions." They all demand a Bible. 1. Liable to be overlooked. 2. Corroborated by other evidence. 3. Trustworthy as far as they go. 4. Liable to misuse. 5. Are roused by the Christian facts. 6. Consistent with each other. 7. All prophetic and not final. 8. All endorsed, purified, liberated, by the Bible. 9. Which to do this

must be inspired of God. 10. Both they and the Bible disclose a common trend.

SECTION II. OUR ACTUAL BIBLE, ... 71
1. Is a growth. 2. Its method historical and biographical. 3. Its Old Testament calls for the New Testament. 4. Its New Testament is to be read into the Old. 5. Christ's use of the Old Testament. 6. The vital thought that makes the Bible one unique book. 7. Everywhere the trend.

CHAPTER III

THE EXPERIENTIAL ARGUMENT

SECTION I. THE CONTENTS OF THE CHRISTIAN EXPERIENCE, ... 114
1. This experience a fact. 2. It is co-ordinated with biblical facts. 3. Its worth as an argument for inspiration. 4. Its evidence as a supplementary fact.

SECTION II. THE WORTH OF THIS EXPERIENCE AS AN ARGUMENT, ... 123
1. Its weight with those not Christians. 2. May not alone satisfy investigators. 3. Subordination of spiritual to intellectual method. 4. The biblical redactors.

SECTION III. CHRISTIAN EXPERIENCE AS A SAFEGUARD, 131
1. The "inward blessing" and the written word. 2. A saving restraint.

SECTION IV. WHAT IS INVOLVED IN THE CHRISTIAN EXPERIENCE, ... 135
1. In it a demand for inspiration as a fit thing. 2. As an expected thing. 3. As an authoritative thing. 4. As a satisfactory thing. 5. The testimony is unique and universal in each of these respects.

CHAPTER IV

THE WARRANTED DEDUCTIONS

SECTION I. WHAT WE ARE WARRANTED TO EXPECT, . . 150
  1. As to an inspiring Spirit. His testimony to inspiration.

SECTION II. THE CHARACTER OF MEN, ... 153
  1. The testimony of the men he inspires as to their own inspiration. Their testimony to the inspiration of other inspired men. 2. Our Lord's testimony. His promise and the claimed fulfillment.

SECTION III. THE GENERAL COURSE OF DEVELOPMENT, . 166
  1. Development of the inspired facts and their record.

CHAPTER V

THE HUMAN AND THE DIVINE ELEMENTS

SECTION I. THE HUMAN ELEMENT, ... 175
  1. The personality of the writers. 2. The signs showing the time when they wrote. 3. This element not disquieting, but assuring. 4. Human element necessary in order to the divine. 5. Human element a strength and not a weakness. 6. Everywhere the trend.

SECTION II. THE DIVINE ELEMENT, ... 190
  1. Divine record of ordinary things. 2. Of extraordinary things. 3. Divine selection of fit men to inspire. 4. Peculiar prophetic inspiration needed. 5. Parallel divine and human trend.

CHAPTER VI

DIFFICULTIES AND CONFIRMATIONS

SECTION I. ANTHROPOMORPHISM, ... 206

CONTENTS

Section II. Chronology, ... 208

Section III. Various Readings, ... 216

Section IV. Unintelligibleness, ... 218

Section V. Unfulfilled Prophecy, ... 219

Section VI. Discrepancy of View, ... 230

Section VII. Topographical Discrepancies, ... 233

Section VIII. Alleged Savagery, ... 239

Section IX. Continuous Revelation, ... 242

INSPIRATION CONSIDERED AS A TREND

CHAPTER I

THE SUBJECT STATED

HERE is a book called "The Bible." For it a very peculiar claim is entered. It is held by some that its statements, not only of ordinary but of extraordinary facts, have a degree, more or less complete, of divine sanction and inspiration.

**Section I.
The Questions Involved**

If, indeed, God has had to do with this book as with no other, that fact is of the utmost importance. To make such a claim if unwarranted is a terrible mistake—a mistake only equalled by the rejection of the claim if the book is really inspired of God. On this claim, since it comes to every man living in a Christian land, some decision is to be made. Every man has a very serious responsibility, not only for doing something about this claim, but for doing it wisely and rightly. If, indeed, this book had received as yet but little attention, it were another thing. If it were an obscure publication, by writers little known in any age of the world, one might with some show of reason wait for a time. If it had made no mark on any generation, one in a busy world might perhaps hold himself in some suspense about examining it. But here is a book so remarkable that foremost minds have devoted long years to its critical study, and have come to see that it so far exceeds as to supersede other books on its peculiar theme. It has swayed the best men. It has met deep perplexities. It has awakened sublime aspirations. It has inspired useful lives. It has assuaged human sorrows. It has kindled strongest hopes. It has made men brave and women pure.

Nor has it done these things alone for any one class of mankind. True, it is the peculiar heritage of a great number of thoughtful, devout, and scholarly men, who have brought to it disciplined minds, accurate habits of investigation, and the best culture of the schools. But it has had an immense hold, as well, upon the millions of those strong, stalwart middle-class men; those men who with clear heads are not likely to be, on any large scale, for any considerable time, very wrong in their better judgments; those men who are the best class when arrayed as a jury for deciding upon evidence submitted to them; the class which has been foremost in prosecuting moral reforms and producing the great moral leaders of mankind. These men never would have taken up this book had they not believed that in some sense or other God has had to do with it as with no other book. These men have held it to be in some way a divinely inspired volume. Such a profound conviction, while not a decisive evidence, warrants us in demanding for this claim at least a fair degree of attention.

THE SUBJECT STATED

Under these circumstances, the burden of proof for the rejection of this claim clearly lies with its opponents. For here is the book. It exists. Somebody wrote it. Its existence is a fact in literature to be explained on some reasonable theory before it can reasonably be rejected. Its influence as well as its existence is a thing for which one is bound to give some account if the book is to be discarded. One must work logically in any process of denial and rejection. The book has had such a prodigious influence on the world that no man may regard it as a foolish volume. In it is a potency of some kind. It is the most widely printed and largely read book upon the planet today. What is it that makes it the most living book in human thought, gathering millions every seventh day to study its contents, to hear its exposition, and to learn by one day's teachings how to live on all the other days of the week? Has any other book such vital force? What is it that gives it such hold on the best portions of the human race?

These men all believe that, in some sense, in some way, divine authority attaches to the Bible. This does not prove its unique claim. But it shows that, if a man is to decline to accept the book, he must do so for some good logical reason given only after examination of the book itself, and after carefully weighing these claims made for it by this great body of men. These men who receive it, many of them, are prayerful men. They believe in God. They have moral as well as intellectual standards of measurement. They are wont to decide questions involving morals, in part at least, by a spiritual instinct. They have a sharpened spiritual appetite and they know bread from stone. They do not gather grapes from thorns.

With these men one should differ with great hesitation on a question of such importance. The strong probabilities are in favor of a true spiritual trend in the course they take on this matter. Their conviction should be given due weight. In examining this question of an inspired volume, we should act not only with reference to good men, but also as in the presence of God. If it be not true that these claims can be substantiated, there is still left us a belief that God is, and that most likely he is the answerer of prayer. And the wisdom that is necessary he can impart. There can be no matter over which one should spend himself in more urgent and agonizing supplication than over doubts which may come in about a divine revelation to man. Only after earnest prayer for the Enlightening Spirit can a man reasonably reject such a book as the Bible. For the deepest moral instincts and the most fundamental convictions of the human heart as they are stirred within us are to have a voice in deciding upon these claims. Our whole complex selfhood is to be consulted. Our very fears are to come into play. It would be the saddest of all sad things if it should turn out that the book we have received as from God is, after all, only a fortuitous assemblage of myths; a series of mistakes gathered about a mistake. And we should be even worse off if the book should turn out to be a composite of part fable and part fact. In that case it would be worse for us than if it were a cheat; for a cheat detected can be dismissed. But a book that should mix miracle with myth and fiction with fact would furnish the worst of perplexities to honest souls. Better no guide than one who does not know the way. Our own doubts are enough without his. If reduced to guessing, we can do our own. But it would, indeed, be a thing to say in tearful tones, that this book after all may mislead. All that is best in humanity would be forced into mourning, and all that is worst would inevitably receive impetus from such a decision. A vast deal is at stake. We shall have lost not only faith in the book as from God, but faith in humanity. Its fairest and best portion, its men whose moral instincts are the highest, who are most tender and reverent in their inquiries are, in that case, wrong. They are not simply wrong on one point, but vitally wrong in their most earnest religious convictions. The wrong pulsates in every heart-beat and passes through every artery and vein of the moral nature. These men have believed that the book differs in kind and in authority from all other books. They take its texts as the proof of doctrine and as the law of the Christian life; and without always expressly defining what they mean by inspiration, they consciously or unconsciously give the book substantially the homage due to the claim. If they are wrong, not only is it a rejection of a book to which they must no longer give their respect and reverence, but the damage to all their best ideals of human nature is something immense. The best men in the line of the best things are deceived. Humanity at its highest is the sport of accident, the victim of mistake; possibly, also, of imposture. It may be said that the scientific method is careless of results if it can only discover the truth. But can any man afford, in deciding what is the truth, to refuse care about the results? By the fruit, in part at least, we know the tree.

Nor is this all. If there has been given to us a revelation from God we owe him a duty therefor. We are, if this book is really a Divine revelation, not only striking a blow at humanity by its rejection, but we are doing a great wrong to God. A mistake here is a sin. The wrong to him, on the one hand, of receiving what he has not given, can be matched only by the other wrong of rejecting what he has actually inspired. Anyway, there is vast responsibility for doing either the one or the other.

It may be urged that many plain Christians have never been over the whole ground of the evidence for believing the Bible to be inspired of God. But do they need to do so? They have a kind of growing proof which comes from acting upon the belief. They will not be obliged to give up what they have discovered of its value and potency in order to be fair in their dealing with it. They must not be required to begin *de novo*, as if the book were not true, and then start to prove it to be from God. In mathematics, is a man to be asked to empty himself of all his knowledge gained by forty years' use of the multiplication table? He began in childhood by learning it as an exercise of memory. He assumed it to be correct. And for all these forty years, in daily use of it, he never found it to fail of being true. Here comes a man and expresses a doubt about its accuracy. There have been men who made this challenge. They have bidden this accountant give up forty years of experience and prove that two and two make four! He will do nothing of the sort. The one to produce evidence is the objector, not the believer in the multiplication table. He has employed it in his work every day, and in the most practical of all ways, that of experimental use, he has found it trustworthy. He now stands by his proved work. He has amassed proofs. He is sure about that multiplication table. It would be strangely unfair to himself, to his science, to all the interests involved, for him to start by surrendering his well-founded conviction. Let the objector start with doubt. Let him enter on his proofs *de novo*, if he has any to offer. The burden is clearly on his shoulders. The man who has studied the book and practised its precepts and yielded himself to its spirit is certain that it is like no other book. He may have little analytical power. Into discussions about the degree, kind, method, of divine influence exerted on the writers, he may or may not enter. But exactly in proportion to his spiritual experience of the unique power of the book will be his regard for it, and his belief that God has had to do with it as with no other book. In such cases we may admit a predisposition like that of a mathematician for his science. The mathematician would claim that

INSPIRATION CONSIDERED AS A TREND

thereby he was not the worse but the better judge of a mathematical problem. There are many side questions appealing to the reason. But the main appeal of the Bible is to the spiritual and moral nature. And therefore the moral and spiritual man is the better fitted for a just decision. When experience in mathematical science is a bar to fair judgment in case of a volume on mathematics, then a long and strong religious experience may be considered a hindrance to the examination of a volume on morals and religion like the Bible. A sympathetic interest in its object and its methods, as well as a knowledge of its whole scope, is needed. There is to be exercised, not so much on single texts as upon the great comprehensive idea of the book, the most careful moral as well as intellectual judgment before a man can honestly reject the claim of its inspiration.

Perhaps it will be found that there are vastly more difficulties in discarding its true and proper inspiration than in accepting the simplest solution that is possible, viz., that it is God's book through man and for man. Perhaps the knowledge of the great controlling thought of the book may make it easier to believe that God had to do with it than that it is merely a product even of the most exalted human genius. We may find that all our ways of accounting for it are needed in their grand sum. This is what many think. If they are right, it is a great truth on which they have fallen. If they are wrong, it is a great mistake they have made. Either way, the decision is of immense importance.

THE SUBJECT STATED

This importance attaching to a decision in either direction is at once obvious from the inevitable results. Let it be true that the book is not inspired by God, but only by human genius however exalted, and certain inferences cannot but be drawn from the fact. Let it be true that the Hebrew race, foremost and purest in all ethical and spiritual ideas, have in this book presented the world with a literature chiefly religious, but standing on a basis, so far as authority is concerned, that is only human—not otherwise inspired than are all human productions save in degree—and there are direct inferences of a sort wholly different from those warranted by a belief that it has both human and divine inspiration. Let the Old Testament come to be regarded as only a collection of annals, songs, prophecies, and proverbs, having indeed far greater value than those of surrounding nations, but with no special and peculiar endorsement of God, then it has no other and higher authority than that always accorded to human productions of great worth. It is of man only, precisely as all other books are of man only. Every man feels the debasement of authority, the lowering of tone, the prodigious difference of the conception. The view narrows rather than broadens. For no view can be so broad, so strong, so lofty, so sustained as that which finds in this book a sanction, a superintendence, an inbreathing not accorded to any other. Let the Old Testament be regarded as merely an outgrowth of human development, and it still has religious value; but we must take this currency at a fearful discount. Its characters, "real or imaginary," will still serve the intellectual world "to point a moral and adorn a tale." The words of Scripture can still be gracefully quoted to round out a period. They can be a happy classical allusion. The old-time Hebrews can serve us in literary work as do the old-time heroes of the Grecian story. They can be used to illustrate any exalted idea we have ourselves originated. We can quote from the Old Testament exactly as from the Koran—when it is an endorsement of our own belief. It will be among the sheaves that do obeisance to the one of our own binding. But authority is gone from any declaration it may contain. Indeed, we judge it by the standard of our own ideas, approving or condemning as it favors or does not favor our own conclusions. It would be claimed by some who would dispense with any special divine authority, to be a matter of comparatively little importance whether Abraham or Moses, whether Elijah or David ever really existed. It would be claimed that the moral impression is just the same on the world whether they did or did not live.

And yet it is only fair to say that some men holding very lightly by the inspiration of Scripture, do not go to this length, but claim that at least the historical accuracy of the Old Testament must be preserved. For they see that these lives and these acts of the old Hebrew worthies are a long series of preparatory events, and that any denial of them spoils the cumulative moral impression of the series, and that thus the most important part of the moral influence would be lost. For it is not alone in the individuality of the lives in which these grand heroes set forth some virtue that they are worth most to the world, but because they are as links of a chain, stones of an arch, lines of a figure, parts of a whole.

Nor is this all. Take any one individual with his characteristic work out of the series for a moment, that you may hold up that man as an object-lesson and his work as an example, and it does make a vast difference to the impression whether the person described as doing the work is fictitious or real, and whether his alleged deeds are fancies or are facts. The Hegelian method of treating history was the "impressionist fashion." The fact was held to be of little worth. The important thing was the impression on the minds of succeeding generations. It was asked why we might not ignore the biblical facts, but retain the principle involved in them. Maurice himself, touched by the Hegelian phase of thinking, when writing to his son who had asked him "whether a legend which appealed to conscience might not produce the same good results as an actual fact," was obliged to answer in the negative. "For," said he, "if God reveals his ideas to us, the revelation must be through facts." "I believe," he continues, "that all is good just so far as it tests facts; and all is bad and immoral which introduces the notion that it signifies little whether they turn out to be facts or no." If it shall turn out that there are conceptions of facts and classes of events which need inspiration for any fair record of them, then the doctrine of a divine inspiration could not be dismissed from the Old Testament without loss both of the facts and of their moral impression.

If we come to the New Testament with our doubts about inspiration, the results are even more obvious. Let it once be held that the Gospels are accidental narratives, taking their shape and presenting their contents as casual fragments; that the Epistles are old letters which by chance have escaped oblivion, and so are valuable only as showing an individual phase of passing religious thought, and the book ceases to have any considerable authority. And doctrine, held on the strength of its statements, must be held loosely and tentatively. Merely human thought never cuts the same circle twice in a century. Its circumference has no more a fixed point than has its changing center. There cannot consistently be any faith save faith in change. There is no steadiness save that of a steady flux in belief. The natural religious instincts are all that remain for guidance; and God himself could make no supernatural revelation that we should be warranted in believing. We have estopped certainty by questioning the best certified Christian facts and doctrines which we can imagine to be given. The lack of inspiration in the New Testament makes what little of it remains to us more perplexing than if it had never been written. For it raises more questions than it solves, and the sifting of probabilities becomes a new and a confusing labor. And yet, if the book is not supernaturally inspired, we must undertake to thread this labyrinth, pitied by others, and most of all pitying ourselves in our doubtful work. It will not be wise to assert very strongly any truth of religion; since the only basis is our own fallibility, and there is no ascertainable standard that is not liable to be altered by our own personality.

But if the opposite of all this is true, there is a new bright world flooded for us by perpetual sunshine. If the book is sanctioned and directed and inbreathed of God, if the human authors of the book in their highest human inspiration were touched and illuminated by a peculiar divine inspiration, then there dawns upon us the happy possibility of having some good degree of definiteness in our religious beliefs. That fact fixed, our search for truth in religion is immensely simplified. We still use our best native powers, but they are working in a new atmosphere, to new advantage, and toward moral certainty as the assured result.

Our inquiry then, is narrowed to these two questions, *viz.:* Is the text of Scripture fairly preserved, and what does the text mean? Reason still has a place, but it is a buttress to the structure built upon the foundation of a divinely authenticated revelation. The moral instincts are still of value. For they are roused into highest activity by the truth and the Spirit of God. But the sovereign judge from whose decision there is no appeal will be this Bible. A multitude of things can now be held very firmly. Not that they are altogether understood. A man's lack of understanding as to how a thing can be so is now seen to be no bar to believing, on the authority of the Bible, that it is so. And thus a man's creed that had been very short and hazy and vacillating while he doubted an inspired Bible, becomes very long and broad, very deep and high, very sure and satisfying, since it has for its authority the inspiration of Holy Scripture. Apart from such authority it is almost presumptuous to hold many a thing which is traditionally received even by those who doubt or deny this supernatural guidance. But the book accepted, to hold less than the large, full, confident truth would be a wrong to God and to one's own self. Fullness of belief, strength of conviction, and the irrevocable yielding of one's intellectual and moral nature to the sway of great Christian facts and doctrines will be secured only in the presence of divine inspiration. In the actual conflict with error the Christian who will do most efficient work is he who wields, with strong heart and steady head and practised hand, "the sword of the Spirit which is the word of God." There will be a decisiveness about the blows he strikes and an assurance that one fights in a winning cause.

And yet, on the other hand, there are devout and scholarly men who claim that much of the prevalent unbelief in the Bible would be at once given up if young men of culture who come to the study of the Bible were met by a less formal demand for the belief in its inspiration. The claim is that the popular prejudice against the book on account of its miraculous incidents, on account of its alleged discrepancies and its undeniable difficulties, would disappear if this claim of its Divine inspiration were modified. It would be possible to gain the assent of men who are not yet spiritually minded, but who mean to be intellectually honest toward the book. As yet they are hindered from believing its religious truths because obliged also to assent to a large number of statements against which they are now rebellious. Afterward, when these men have begun on the moral side of religious inquiry, it is thought they may come to accept statements which are now full of perplexity to them. Some Christian men, loving the Bible themselves but in close sympathy with many who doubt even if they do not deny the inspiration of the Scriptures, have proposed in this way to make the path easier for the perplexed and the troubled.

But it has been urged in reply that no other subject is studied by the surrender of facts; that to give up a part is not anywhere else the best way to gain the whole ; that to meet in this way one class of minds is to unsettle others. It is indeed very true that in arguing with a man on any topic the primary thing is to show him that, believing one thing, he is thereby compelled to go on and believe another truth involved in the one he admits. But that is not to assert that you believe no other truth than the one which you are presenting to him. You do not surrender all else in order to assert something on which you and he agree. Careful thinkers see what is involved in denial. To-day the great question in religious inquiry is of the basis of authority rather than of the method of reasoning. The more legal and logical any mind, the more judicial its cast, the stronger will be its demand for authority in religion. Authentic documents are the necessity of the century for a religion which centers in a great historic person like Jesus Christ. Loose-jointed minds may work in other ways, but trained and scholarly men will insist on documentary evidence as to historic facts; and when some of the facts are supernatural, they will crave supernatural accuracy in the record of them.

Nor is this conviction of the inspiration of the volume needed alone for careful and cultured thinkers. Others as well need this foundation. The great mass of Christian men, men of large common sense, but without classical training, are the ones chiefly needing to be satisfied. They are the bulk of the Christian community. Those who know them the best respect their convictions the most. They are the safest jury with which to entrust moral causes. They are the men mainly addressed by the Bible. For merely scholastic questions they have as little aptitude as they have concern. They believe in the reality of truth. They have mental and moral health enough to believe that the truth can be known. They feel that the Bible is for them. They are convinced that they are able to make up their minds about the truth. They think the book was given them for their salvation from error as well as from sin. They know it as the most democratic of books in this respect. And so, this book, addressing this great and grand class of mankind out from which have come foremost leaders in moral and religious reforms, has an immense hold upon them as an inspired volume. Its Christ sprang from this class of men. Among them he found his apostles and out of their ranks have come his foremost servants the ages through and the world around. These men in their need and their claim are to be regarded. It is to them an almost intuitive truth that a Bible of any considerable worth must have a divine sanction. They instinctively feel that some higher authority than man is needed. This book furnishes it for them. It would take another book with greater miracles clustering about a greater Lord whose utterances were more tender and whose promises were more glorious—if such a book there could be—to convince them by its testimony that this book is not distinctively inspired of God. They feel that it is true. They are sure of its trend. Their moral intuitions are roused and their hearts are capable of a reasoning on such a theme which is as sound as any logic of the head. They know that the whole trend of their best feeling and the whole trend of the book is the same. The key fits the lock.

No argument better satisfies any man's head and heart alike than that of trend. Some of these men may be too impatient of discussion. They may need to be assured that those who enter on the investigation of this subject of inspiration, do so with a friendly rather than an unfriendly purpose; that their own moral intuitions are not to be outraged. These believers cannot give up what they know with the deepest moral knowledge of their souls. They need to be assured that, instead of denying or even setting aside for the time, on the plea of fairness, these moral certainties, we are going to consider candidly these facts of their religious experience. They need to know that we seek also a logical basis, in addition to the experiential proof on which they rightly insist; that the method in which we are to prosecute the inquiry is that of strict induction until we have assembled the facts; that one class of these facts is this very experience. We are to examine also the direct and the indirect teaching of the Scriptures themselves on this subject. The legitimate deductions from all this mass of evidence are to be carefully drawn. And thus we are to gather up all the various and consenting evidences which show that we have not followed " cunningly devised fables " in accepting the Scriptures as the " word of God." These men feel none too strongly the importance of this matter, while all scholarly and devout men call inspiration "the burning question of the hour."

Section II. The Recognition of Trend

In the previous section there was set forth, to some extent, the importance of the subject. And perhaps the difference in the results of the extreme theories of inspiration was dwelt upon sufficiently. But what if there is another side? What if it is of equal importance to look fairly upon the unifying principle which, it may be, runs through all these diverse theories? What if we can discover, not indeed harmony in them, but a certain unity of trend? And what if this principle of trend not only is found in the varying theories of the book, but is also a feature of the Scriptures themselves? All the theories confess to the fact that we have here a most remarkable book in contents, in tone, in trend of thought, and in trend of fact as well. The theories run for a certain distance in the same general direction.

It may be freely granted that their unlikeness is very obvious. But certainly their similarity in some things is worthy of our recognition. What if this likeness as well as this unlikeness is such because the subject of inspiration is one far too wide to be spanned by any single theory? What if each most extreme view explains some things better than any other and yet in turn has its own defects? What if the trend of all the theories is like the trend of all the book? Trend is tendency. It realizes itself in seeking, through present manifestations, its final accomplishment. It is that course in things which goes onward to result, that direction in things which seeks a goal. It may be so strong as to satisfy us completely as to its character and its ends. There is a descriptive definition of God as "that stream of tendency that makes for righteousness." In like manner one might describe inspiration, in one of its aspects, as that tendency in human affairs which makes for divine revelation, the divinely guided record of which is the Bible. And we are to recognize this human tendency in the various theories of inspiration, and also to recognize the divine tendency in the book itself.

There are those who admit only this: that the highest expression of the religious thought of former ages is to be found in this book. In some very general sense they allow that it is a record of the teachings of foremost souls enlightened by the Spirit of God. They say that the book shows great religious genius. But even this restricted view carries with it a vast deal more as a necessary deduction than those who admit so much would willingly allow. But what this admission really involves will be considered farther on.

There are those who claim the verbal inspiration of the book, *i. e.*, the inspiration of its words. These claimants differ widely among themselves; some holding to a mechanical dictation, in which a man is merely an "amanuensis of God," and some insisting that the verbal guidance only preserves the penman from error in expressing his thought. A verbal theory, they say, need not be a mechanical theory.

There are again other men who contend only for the inspiration of the thought by the Spirit of God. And the inspiration of the thought does indeed lift us to a broader moral atmosphere than that of the mere word. And some feel that if they must choose between the two theories, the theory of the inspired thought is the more spiritual, the more logical, the more reliable for us, than that of a merely verbal inspiration.

Others would unite the two theories. They claim that if the inspired thought does not absolutely compel an inspired expression, it clearly points in that direction.

Then there is the dynamical theory of inspiration. It is that the writers of Scripture were suffered to fall into no error or mistake in things affecting moral fact or religious doctrine, though they took their own way of recording facts, even when some of the facts, not especially religious and but incidentally named, were not geographically or historically exact. For religious purposes they are absolutely truthful.

Again, there are those who claim that the series of events are inspired—these only. The teaching which historians, prophets, evangelists, and apostles draw from these inspired events has little or no divine guidance. We have left us nothing other than that which very shrewd and profoundly religious men have seen in them. And thus each age has put its stamp upon the inspired events, seeing them in its own atmosphere and limitations. So that an event, say that of the deluge, has one teaching for the age of Moses, as it looks back to it; another teaching for the age of Joel; and a third for the age of Jesus. It is seen by the eye of Paul and by that of Peter, each putting into it his own personality and imperfection. Neither the thought nor the word has inspired worth; and the narration is simply a water-mark showing the moral or the literary position of an age or of a man.

About each of these theories and others which could be named, some things may be said:

I. It is obvious that each of them, since it has clear and devout thinkers as its advocates, may have in it some element of truth.

II. One of these theories may explain a particular phase of the subject more satisfactorily than any other to some careful inquirer.

III. That seldom is any one theory held in absolute consistency.

Those, for instance, who hold to the most extreme form of verbal inspiration, even when they compare man's work to that of a "pen in the hand of divinity," do not hesitate to point out the fact of the testimony of eye-witnesses in the case of Moses when describing his wilderness journey, and in the case of the apostles when describing the miracles and teachings of the Lord. So too, those who hold to the inspiration of the events as a series ask us to notice the fact that, in some circumstances, other words than those selected in the record would have spoiled the relation of one member of the series to the rest. To us it would seem that the words need to be as carefully chosen sometimes as the events, to be of any worth in the premises. Thus no man is probably quite consistent in his special theory. He extends or contracts it in given cases. In using his theory he transgresses it by a happy inconsistency.

It is the same with the man who insists that the writers are to be regarded chiefly as splendid specimens of lofty human genius. Now and then these biblical writers seem to him to snatch a glance beyond that limitation. Now and then they reach a plane and utter a word that has the tone of the superhuman. The seer sees. The hearer hears words beyond those which are mortal. The theory is forgotten as the words inspire. The man has allowed, in a moment of vision, what he had been loth to admit when the vital eye had become dimmed. Men are sometimes more believing than their unbelief. The natural faculty for believing asserts its potency. And here and there a word, a truth, or a series of events, is more than human on the biblical page.

The frequent and happy inconsistencies of the advocates of any one special theory should teach us that it will be best to hold any theory less in a hard and fast way and more in a way that sees in each and all a trend. It is not necessary to find any common ground of agreement on definite points, but rather to see if each does not contain a truth which the others fail to emphasize, and to note that in them all there is a certain trend of thought.

IV. It is evident also that investigators on this field of inquiry should be careful not to undervalue the results others have reached. No man serves the truth best by showing that all other men are mistaken. Truths are friendly. It is not worth while to discredit all others to get a hearing for one's self. The poorest kinds of arguments on some great themes are those which work toward mutual destructiveness. In the very varieties of theories one may find not indeed a unity of result, but of intention, of tendency, of outlook. They may be approximations. One need not disparage the lesser light another man has brought, nor the different way by which that other man approaches the subject and reaches his end. The argument most convincing to another man may be the least satisfactory to you who hold the same truth with him. But you do not need to bring your superior way into right angles with his. Let it be parallel.

Yours goes farther, as you think. But do not seek at any point on these highest themes to antagonize his view. Members of the same army should not draw swords on each other. We cannot afford in getting at the intellectual form of this singularly broad subject to cultivate antagonisms. The truth may be, and probably is, far broader than any or all of our theories of it. Every man working amid the materials of this problem will help us, if it shall be found presently that the utmost possible for us to do is to establish the fact of trend and to discover which way it leads.

This will not be to attempt the establishment of any new theory of inspiration, but we may be able to show that each theory may have something that the other lacks. Each may cast a sidelight on the subject. He need not be wholly right who by some single view of the theme has opened a new line of thinking. The best views are approximations. And he would be singularly wanting in knowledge of the theme of inspiration who thinks that the last word has been spoken. Let us welcome all that any candid, prayerful, scholarly man has to say. He can hardly discuss the theme at all without contributing, incidentally at least, something that may be worth our notice. There may be great error in his view as a whole, but some subordinate line of remark may be of especial value. Considered as the sole theory of inspiration his view may be utterly untenable. But is it not possible that a theory while failing to cover all the ground may be a contribution as showing a trend? What if all our theories only show which way the truth lies? What if they are indications, prophecies, approaches? All these beginnings show that there is somewhere a goal. They show a belief in something higher than ordinary human genius in certain writings. Perhaps the general direction of all these processes, starting as they do from various sides of the subject, will show by their variety not only the fact of trend, but that trend is the greatest fact of all.

One of our foremost teachers in physics at the close of his series of lectures on "gravitation," was asked by a student whom he had admitted to intimacy, "Do you think, professor, that your arguments have proved gravitation?" "Proved it? No," was the instant answer. "We prove none of these things. We only show which way things tend. The facts look that way." Equally ignorant are we about "sound," about "electricity," and "chemical affinity." Our theories are at best only tentative. They do as working theories. We can see the general trend of scientific thought. We are on the right track; but we have not come to the end. In biology it is the same. See how many have tried to define "life." No two of the great masters agree in their theory of it. Yet all know what it is experimentally. We all know that life is the one thing of which death is the opposite. We know it as the mysterious something that tends to make an organism do what it is plainly intended to do. If we cannot define, we can describe; and all we do is to describe a direction, a tendency in things.

In the great discussion concerning the existence

of God some good thinkers are coming to give credit to all the different arguments as having a certain worth. The argument from design shows a great Designer. But need he be the Infinite and Eternal God? The ontological argument shows a Creator. But may he not be a lesser being than the Almighty One? The argument from the power displayed in the world shows potency beyond all our conception. But was there need of an absolutely Almighty Being to make this wondrous frame of things? How do we know but that less than Infinite Wisdom could have contrived them all? These arguments do not any one of them alone reach an absolute demonstration.

It is the same with the argument that we have a natural, necessary, universal conviction that there is a God. It is the same with the argument that there is a preparation in the mind for receiving the idea of a Supreme Being. Not one of these arguments is destitute of worth. Each one of them has its advocates who must take care not to disparage the arguments of other thinkers. And so it is coming about that a large class of minds—and they not of inferior caliber—look on all these theories chiefly as exhibiting a tendency which is unmistakable. It is not what the arguments have in common that makes them of worth, but it is their very difference which makes this stream of tendency so evidential. As we dwell upon it, this trend becomes the argument of arguments. So satisfying is it that we may well inquire whether it was not intended that various methods of approaching the truth on this matter should be used by different

THE SUBJECT STATED

minds, and thus each of them contribute toward establishing a form of argument stronger than any one or all of them. So that the belief in God becomes satisfactory to a degree impossible in any other way.

Are there any who, because unused to this line of thinking, imagine that we surrender arguments either on the subject of divinity or of divine inspiration for a "mere trend"? But let us remember that a trend may be of the very strongest kind. It may be the most positive evidence of a fact. Take that tendency called the "magnetic trend." All over the surface of the world, as has been said, sweep the lines of magnetic force. They run up toward the Pole of the earth. These lines are the basis of two of the greatest sciences we have. By them we measure the world and the very skies. We venture, because of this trend, across oceans and deserts otherwise impassable. We measure the starry heavens by this same trend. These lines are all run toward a Pole that no man has yet seen, but which must exist. Trend is the strongest possible proof of it. No man in his senses wants any other proof.

It is the same with reference to inspiration. He who ordained that trend should be the best proof of himself has ordained that it should be the best proof of his divine inspiration of the Bible. What if the nature of this divine inspiration is such that when his Spirit comes to man's spirit the law of the manifestation is similar? And thus the trend in our own minds may be but the reflection of that in the Divine mind as shown us in the Divine word.

And so Divine inspiration may be proved to us in the same way as Divine existence. The point to which our human inquiries lead may be that toward which God's word also conducts us. Tendency is the great thing to be noted, alike in the Bible itself and in our study of its pervasive thought. This movement toward a definite point is seen in the fact of its varied methods of utterance. Just here there is a line of evidence toward which many students not quite satisfied with any one theory of inspiration are now looking. This living purpose, this determinative process, this evident seeking for the goal, this active concernment, this whole strong trend of the Bible—these are the facts more satisfactory to many persons than any other proof that the book is from God.

Notwithstanding the difficulty of exact logical definition, the interest felt in this matter of inspiration shows the immense importance attached to the subject. Elsewhere the subjects that deeply interest students are incapable of any other definition than the descriptive one of trend. In biology, no definition of life satisfies any man save him who proposes it. But the thing itself is none the less real because, instead of definition, we must content ourselves in the end with only a description. Our definition of God is always lacking and must be so. Even in nature, we apprehend many a thing we cannot comprehend. That a thing is, may be certain to us, when we do not understand how it is. And all the more important facts in nature, in philosophy, and in religion, are among these things that we can better describe than de-

THE SUBJECT STATED

fine. Such is the case with this subject of Divine inspiration, the importance of which can hardly be overestimated. It is one of the "burning questions" of the age. From every side we welcome all truth upon it. Every line of investigation which promises to give us any help is gladly employed and all results carefully accepted.

It will be, then, our pleasant task to look closely, even if briefly, at some of the chief methods open to us in examining this whole subject. Perhaps we shall find everywhere, amid various ways of investigation, an increasing proof of trend.

CHAPTER II

THE GATHERED MATERIAL

Section I. Our Natural Intuitions

THE inductive method of investigating any subject starts with the attempt to ascertain the facts. It asks, not what we should think they would be, but what they are. It proposes no theory. It gathers facts as so much material on which subsequently we may work.[1] It proposes to see these facts as nearly as possible in the dry light of a scientific method. It is true that a human eye must see these facts, and every observer has that which astronomers in their observations are obliged to take into account, viz., the "personal equation." Every man's eye has its peculiarity, for which in each case due allowance must be made. And there is a wide difference in the number of facts which different minds deem sufficient to constitute a basis that will warrant a con-

---

[1] "Induction," says Whately, "is sometimes employed to designate the process of investigation and of collecting facts, and sometimes the deducing of an inference from them." In this part of the discussion, we are to investigate the facts of our human nature which show at once our need and our capacity to receive an inspired revelation; and in a subsequent section we seek to ascertain the facts as found in our "Written Bible." Certain inferences may be drawn in the processes of investigation. But the "Warranted Deductions" are given a separate chapter. "Scientific induction is a constant interchange of induction and deduction." Definition in "Standard Dictionary."

clusion. There is the discount always to be made for the judgment of different men as to the importance to be allowed to a given fact; and there is also the danger that unimportant facts will not be excluded and pertinent facts will not be given due weight. The method has its obvious limitations and disadvantages, even when applied to physical science. But when we come to the moral realm of things, the limitations and the dangers multiply. Prejudice and passion, partial intellectual training and imperfect moral judgment cannot but influence men. It is often, for instance, a difficult thing to decide whether a human mind as shown by a given book exhibits an ability amounting to genius. And how much greater is the difficulty arising from a man's own peculiarity, whether of temperament or of training, of deciding in an absolutely scientific way, by induction alone, whether the book we call the Bible exhibits the Divine mind working through the human genius in such a way and to such a degree as to warrant us in calling the book a Divine inspiration. The facts will have different weight with different minds, and with the same mind at different times. They will be differently marshaled and sorted. One mind will estimate them by number, another by quality. There are closely built minds, and there are loosely knit minds; judicial minds and minds discursive. Above all, there are men who are nimble and men who are slow in their moral methods and judgments; men who are unpractised gunners in moral warfare; and other men whose accuracy and precision show the result of careful training as they have used themselves in moral warfare amid the conflict of great principles.

These considerations do not tend toward the unfortunate conclusion that our human knowledge is unreliable. They show that one particular way of arriving at moral results may need to be compared and corrected by other methods of investigation; just as the eye sometimes needs to be corrected by the ear, and the sense of smell by that of touch. The inductive method of inquiry is one, and is only one, of the ways of studying the subject before us; a way with its own limitations and weaknesses.[1] But it has also its value and its potency among the several ways of ascertaining the truth. Let us use it as best we may in this part of our discussion on the question of inspiration.

It is a fact that Christianity exists as a religion in the world. It is likewise a fact that, for us, in these later centuries, this Christian religion stands closely connected with the existence of a book popularly called the New Testament. Says Bruce, "If the Gospels were to be lost, or all faith in their truth to perish, Christianity as a distinctive type of religion would perish." It is clear that for those accepting this book as an authority—an authority in the same sense as we accept certain well-known histories as authorities—there is found a secure basis on which we can begin in our inquiries on inspiration. And we might ask what the book says, directly, of its own inspiration, and

---

[1] "Induction can ordinarily only give us no more than probable conclusions, because we can never be sure that we have collated all instances." Definition in "Standard Dictionary."

what it assumes in its utterances. We might ask what its tone, its manner, and its bearing are. We might ask what such facts recorded in such a fashion clearly involve. We could obtain a good degree of certainty on this question by seeing what play is given to the human genius of the writers; and we could also ask whether there is not sometimes manifested over and above this a conspicuous element which indicates a higher hand than that of man. We might not yet be ready to give any exhaustive definition of inspiration; for the inductive method expressly waits for the utmost possible gathering of material before it gives actual statements of the law that governs all the facts. But from such an acknowledged basis, it would be possible and even necessary to recognize a degree of divine guidance and endorsement. We may own facts when a full theory of them is not yet warranted. We may mark the fact of a trend even when we do not follow it to a conclusion. The facts may warrant us in looking to the east for the sun, even though the horizon is not yet flecked with the colors that show distinctly its rising beams.

But there are those who do not allow us this basis. They want to go farther back for the facts. Very well. Then we retreat one step, and we get back to the religion out of which Christianity, as all admit, historically sprang. Judaism is certainly a historic religion. It exists; and it existed before Christianity. The main facts of Jewish history are sure. Such a nation as the Hebrews certainly appeared on the earth and did a definite work, and disseminated a definite set of ideas among the nations. It filled a distinct place, as it occupied for centuries a land central to all the ancient civilizations. It connected itself, historically, in one direction with "the youthful world's gray fathers," who were its boast and its model. It had a lawgiver who gave a series of legal institutes that are the basis of the common law of the foremost centuries. The facts of the existence of such a nation and its mission, both legal and religious, and of its peculiar influence on the world, are as sure as the existence of the sun in the heavens. And further: just as Christianity is absolutely connected for us with a certain book called the New Testament, so Judaism is connected for us unalterably with the facts of a book called the Old Testament. The two books being other than they are, the two religions were other than they are. These are basal facts. As each book stands connected with each religion, so the two books and the two religions stand connected with each other. There is therefore a four-fold basis which ought to be a satisfactory warrant. It is such for a vast number of inductive thinkers. And at another point in this discussion this basis is to be legitimately used.

But there are those who would go back farther yet. Very well; we will do it. Only one step farther is possible. We go back to those "primitive beliefs," those "original intuitions," those "warranted assumptions," which some practised thinkers claim to be basal to any thought whatsoever, on both intellectual and moral questions.

They are just what the "axioms" are in geometry, or the multiplication table is in arithmetic. Axioms in geometry are formalized natural beliefs about space and number and quantity. Clearly stated and clearly seen, they carry their own conviction. They cannot be otherwise than they are. They are found, on working upon them, to be trustworthy. They become verified when once they are assumed. In exactly the same way when we turn to the intellectual and moral realm of things we have "primitive convictions." These are "natural and necessary truths." By the five senses we get, in some unexplained way, to the conviction of an external world in which the "primitive truths" of space and number and quantity are actual existences. Exactly so, by consciousness—the contents of the mind looked in upon by itself—we get at those moral and intellectual "intuitions," those "original convictions," those "primary truths," which are involved in all the moral and intellectual workings of the human mind and soul. For the soul does its work in a realm of things as real as is the material. "Whatever," says Mill, "is known to us by consciousness is known beyond the possibility of question." And of these "axioms" in the moral realm we are as absolutely certain as of the axioms in geometry. If indeed there were any difference in the two classes of certainties, the certainty in the sphere of mind would be more abundantly proved. For we are more sure of the mind that knows than of the thing known to the mind through the senses. And while we may have been occasionally deceived about the things we thought we saw or heard, yet as to our thinking about them, we were not deceived. We know that we thought about the things.

These mental and moral facts are the most thoroughly proven facts we know. To doubt them is to doubt thought itself. These "axiomatic truths" are natural, necessary, and universal, as related to the realm of physical things. Once let the human mind clearly see them and they are self-evident. In like manner, let there be a distinct and unobstructed view of these "axiomatic moral convictions," these "primary principles of moral judgment," and they justify themselves. For they have the same three marks by which we test such truths, viz., the marks of naturalness, of necessity, and of universality,

What are these moral intuitions? So far as they bear upon the matter now under discussion, they are these:

I. The belief in self : *i. e.*, the belief in one's self as having one's own body and one's own mind. Our body is separated from the mass of matter and our souls from the mass of soul. We are ourselves.

II. There is a belief in substance outside of our own bodies, and in mind outside of our own minds. Philosophy has attempted to explain how we get at our belief in an external world, whether of matter or mind. The various theories are usually held by careful students as not perhaps so defective in kind as in measure. The ladder ascends in the right direction, but it is too short. The last rung of it is just beyond our ken. The final step toward a conclusion is not the logical one of the reason, but it is the logical one of the intuition. We are so made as to assume the existence of the outside world. It is the conviction less of the reason and more of the intuition. For intuitions are axiomatic to reason and they make reasoning possible. We have to believe in matter outside of our body, and also in reasoning minds outside of our mind. Reasoning involves a standard with which comparison is made in some other mind than our own. We assume other thinking than that of "the me within us."

III. There is an intuitional belief in "the true and the false." We are ushered into a scheme of things in which these distinctions exist. We do not make them but find them here when we come. We assume them as existing in our own and in other minds as a law of judgment to be by us applied; and as having also a real existence outside of our minds. "The true" is what agrees with a rule or standard truth more or less clearly perceived. "The false" is also as real as is the true; and it is that which disagrees with the standard. Ten thousand times men have been deceived as to what particular things are true or false. But the things were judged to be true or false at the time; and when the mistake was discerned, the label was simply changed to the other object. The new judgment was on a new statement of the facts; so that it was still an adjudgment about "the true and the false." The mind believes that the true is knowable, and persists in seeking it notwithstanding all former mistakes. It insists that the trouble was not in its decision, but in the mistaken presentation of the alleged facts at the bar of the mind. The court decides on the evidence produced. If the evidence is false or even partial, the verdict in the case is as defective as is the evidence. The reality of the "true and the false" as a distinction to be made is not invalidated by any mistake of the witnesses on the stand. In any case there is a decision, and this means that the law exists and is acted upon by the judge.

IV. There is an intuitive belief in "the right and the wrong." There is the assumption of a law, agreement with which is the right and disagreement with which is the wrong. This "law" or "standard" or "principle according to which we instinctively judge," we do not make. Our consciences simply recognize it as existing. A good many things tend toward hindering the action of the conscience, exactly as in the case of the reason. But, getting down into the soul of man, we find conscience always there. However deflected, restrained, or limited, the fact that we are susceptible of being thus influenced, so far from suggesting doubt, confirms belief in it as an original principle, as a natural endowment. Men will differ about what things are right, as they do about what things are reasonable. All that we need now to notice is that they make the distinction, even when they do it erroneously. A man's conscience may have been trained to act narrowly and on only a very few things. There is said to be a tribe of Laplanders who will steal without compunction, except when a bit of reindeer skin is thrown over an object. Then, and on that thing, conscience binds them. If it binds them on one thing, that fact shows conscience as existing. And such a conscience, making its distinction of "the right and the wrong" in one thing, shows what it would do if allowed larger range and if exercised about other things. The fact that the "sense of the right and the wrong" is anywhere employed is all that is needed here and now in this discussion.

V. Equally instinctive is the idea of a God who is the standard of the true and the standard of the right. There are reasons of prodigious strength that would hinder a sinful race from believing in a holy and just God. But the conviction holds. It cannot, for any considerable number of men, be beaten down. It has been strangely perverted. Gods many and lords many have been invented to take the place of the original monotheistic conviction. But all the old nations had more or less distinctly the idea of the one God. Arguments from causation, arguments from design, arguments from moral law and moral results, all go a certain way toward the proof, or rather toward dissipating the counter arguments which human guilt, in its frantic desire to deny him, have devised. Argument meets objection. But the argument needs also the help of the "natural instinct," of the "inward conviction," of "the moral persuasion," of the "original handwriting of God testifying to himself." The attempt to prove by mere argument the bare existence of God may fail. So too may fail the effort to find the merely characterless existence of God as an original instinct of man. The instinct is a conviction as to a moral God, who has moral qualities as well as mere existence. He is a fact, not only in the region of mind, but in that of soul as well. He dwells not only in the sphere of thought and will, but in the realm of the moral world. His existence is not to be conceived of as apart from the sphere of the right and wrong. It is a holy God whom good men crave and evil men fear, and all men in the clearest moments of moral insight must own.

VI. The idea of immortality is also a natural belief. Arguments of vast weight have been advanced. They almost reach the goal of proof. They are sufficiently strong to warrant men in acting upon them. But after all the innate conviction is the one evoked by these arguments. We are prepared to believe in immortality. Death seems to interrupt life, but the superficial argument that "death ends all" satisfies only those who want it true that they do not live forever. The instinctive feeling remains. In his book "Scarabs," Dr. Myer, the Egyptologist, tells us that the doctrine of the immortality of the soul was an "advanced instinct of humanity." He says:

It is a curious phase of archaic Egyptian thought, that the farther we go back in our investigations of the origins of its religious ideas, the more ideal and elevated they appear as to the spiritual power of the unseen world. Idolatry made its greatest advance subsequent to the epoch of the Ancient Empire, and progressed until it finally merged itself into the animalism of the new empire and the gross paganism of the Greeks and Romans.

THE GATHERED MATERIAL

The intuition is not only incited to act by the rational nature, but by other parallel intuitions. We ourselves know ourselves to be spiritual in the core of our being. The moral conviction of a moral God with whom we have to do, is closely allied to this natural belief in immortality. We carry with us when we die our moral personality. And this parallel conviction is corroborative of immortality.

There are beginnings of moral action engendering such spontaneous hopes, such vital and necessary expectations of future blessing, that they would need some express revelation from heaven to forbid them were they untrue. The leading is not misleading. Intellectual powers, going on toward their perfected working, moral processes, begun in each to-day and demanding a to-morrow for their completion, are not to be blasted by the incident of death to the body—the body which has survived unharmed greater changes than death itself. These convictions give force to reasoning, since the healthful reason loves to reach in another way, as nearly as possible, the convictions held by the soul as its original endowment. The mind declares concerning itself that it possesses primary thoughts that are undying. Other things may be transient. These truths once seen, these original thoughts once beginning to give their peculiar thrill to the human soul, demand, expect, and prophesy, an immortality in which their eternal expansiveness shall find due scope.

VII. The last of these primary convictions needing to be named for this discussion is that of a *final judgment.* Whether it is a judgment "day" or a judgment "period" no intuition can tell us. There is no doubt of a primitive feeling of accountability to God. It has been, in its development, sadly distorted. The conviction has been used to awaken a craven rather than a holy fear. The abuse of the feeling of accountability has made men rebel against the idea, and fortify their rebellion with whatsoever of reasoning they could command. And so reasons for and against this culminating accountability have been given. The order of all orderly things, and equally the disorder and confusion of the moral world about us, have been used to show that a judgment is needed. There is a conviction that things will culminate, that God must be met, that stewardship is to be ended, probation to be closed, and results summed up in a final judgment. The inward conviction never gets due voicing for itself until it claims that, as a subject of moral government, man must render final account to him who stands at its head as sovereign Judge.

Some would say that this is less an original conviction and more a mood of mind preparatory to the revealed announcement of the fact; an aptitude expectant of the idea, so that it is instantly recognized when once declared. But this way of conceiving of the genesis of the idea differs from the other only by taking into account the obscurations and hindrances that result from human sin. The rubbish removed, the vein of native gold is revealed which elsewhere comes frequently to the surface. The conviction that there is One who ever observes, ever rules, and will reward and punish, is another form in which this intuitive belief manifests itself. There is a Judge. Then there is a judgment. The ideas are connected. The one helps the other, as parallel thereto. The broken and distorted image of God needs rectification by reviving the original instinct; and in like manner the intuitive energy that makes for a final judgment as a belief, is evoked and clarified by the removal of all hindrances, through the aid of a Christian revelation.

About all these native and original convictions a few things need to be considered.

1. They are liable to be overlooked. However native, spontaneous, and universal they may be in themselves, this must be remembered, that self-knowledge is the one thing most difficult to obtain. If the proper study of mankind is man, it is still a fact that thousands never do actually make a study of their own consciousness. However universal any one of these convictions may be, if a man does not look within he will not see it. And those who begin this study of their own intuitions may not be able at first to distinguish those that are spontaneous from those that seem to be the result of education only. And, when seen, some persons may not tabulate them rightly; while others, through lack of facile language, may not give them the adequate expression. In a busy life, so many things outside of our own consciousness claim attention, that the contents of one's own mind may not be observed until attention has been called to them by some other man's report of his

consciousness. When we call these convictions universal, we do not say that all men are always conscious of them; but that, when they are made known, either by our own thought or by the suggestion of other men's convictions, there is a quick answer in response which every human soul is ready to give. The fact of the liability of these primitive and positive convictions to be overlooked is very suggestive as to the need of some further enlightenment of man by revelation.

2. Intuitions can be corroborated by evidence. The multiplication table, taken at first entirely on trust, by sheer force of memory, has been corroborated by the mathematical calculations of all who work at figures. And in like manner these moral intuitions are shown to be primitive along the whole course of moral history, as men have used, and even as they have misused them. Rawlinson says:

> The historic review lends no support to the theory that there has been a uniform growth and progress of religions from fetichism to polytheism and from polytheism to monotheism. In most of the religions the monotheistic idea is most prominent at first, and gradually becomes obscured and gives way to a polytheistic corruption. The facts point to a primitive religion from without, and then a gradual clouding of the primitive religion everywhere unless it were among the Hebrews.

Says Max Müller:

> The monotheistic intuition is inseparable from the conception of religion, and we find traces of it in all places and all times; and this monotheistic conviction is always

accompanied by faith in the persistence of the human personality after death.

Says Rev. George Owen:

The old classics of China show a wonderful knowledge of God. The founders of the Chinese race believed in an omniscient, omnipotent, and omnipresent God, the moral Governor of the world and the impartial Judge of man.

Livingstone says of tribes in the interior of Africa: "They have clear ideas of a supreme God." Testimonies of this kind could be quoted from anthropologists, which would fill many pages. It is true that some learned writers have asserted that polytheism and fetichism were primitive beliefs. But, going a little farther back, they would be obliged to confess to the fact of the more ancient faith. The trend now differing from that forty years ago is toward a belief in God, in a moral government and in a judgment, as the earliest convictions of mankind. And here too is manifested the fact that there is abundant room for a new revelation which shall retrace the old letters, shall clear the moss from the half-effaced words, and restore the original handwriting of God to the freshness and beauty of the original inscription. Says a writer not believed to be friendly to the Bible, in "Articles of the Negative Creed," as quoted by the "Contemporary Review": "A revelation attended by prophecies and miracles is a conceivable proposition, and might teach us that which otherwise we could never know."

3. These intuitions are trustworthy as far as

they go.[1] They are, indeed, but rudiments. They are only the alphabet that makes a written literature a possibility. As a complete religion they would be a manifest failure. They tell us something of great use, when there is also power supplied to overcome the inertia brought about by the sinfulness and weakness of our common humanity. They have no hint of helpfulness when we have done a wrong, or have fallen into any feebleness through infirmity or evil. They are trustworthy deliverances of consciousness as to primitive truths; but they lack potency, just where we most need it, to make them executive for our highest moral good. They are sure points for starting; but they do not insure the gaining of the prize at the other end of the course.

4. These intuitions, however clear in themselves, are liable to be confused by us in our using of them. The axioms of geometry do not insure the correct demonstration by the pupil. He may employ them wrongly. The mind is sometimes deflected in its moral reasoning by unknown prejudices. We are less fair than we had thought ourselves. There is not due allowance for our own personal equation. Other principles than those of the moral nature come into antagonism. The vol-

---

[1] Commenting on the remark of Morrison, that our religious beliefs will soon be "a pious hope rather than a reasoned judgment," and also, upon Renan's remark that religious belief "will die out slowly, undermined by scientific education," Benjamin Kidd in "Social Evolution," says: "These beliefs must remain to the end a characteristic feature. These religious phenomena are among the most persistent." Indeed, the main value of Kidd's discussion is his claim for the reality of the religious sentiment and for what it involves and promises.

untary nature may overrule the ethical. Will may be pitted against God, and passion against conscience. There may be the cross-action of mingling and also of opposing motives. There are cyclones on the ocean, in which mariners say that the wind seems to blow from every quarter at once. No trend, as has been said, is more sure in nature than that of the magnet to the Pole; and yet there are magnetic currents and there are deflections which, unless known and taken into account, would work harm to any ship. She may follow her compass to her ruin, if the deflections are not studied. Nevertheless the compass is an essential thing. Let us give it all honor. We do not esteem it less because of the well-known magnetic deviations. So that, by what these intuitions declare, and equally by their liability to be warped from certainty in our actual use of them, they call for something outside of themselves by which we may study them the better. Beside the true compass, the mariner carries also his true chart, with all the currents, alike of the terrestrial and the magnetic oceans, carefully described; and with all the allowances that must be made for safe navigation carefully set down.

And herein, again, is the need of revelation clearly manifest. The intuition in some minds may need liberation from the self-will or from the wrong reasoning of the individual man. There are tides of popular feeling that eddy about each man's personal life. The brighter and more active the mind, the quicker it is seized upon and dominated by the age-spirit. Always some wind is blowing over the particular continent on which one lives his mental and moral life. And the demand is clear for some rectification, for some outside help, in restoring polarity, in insuring against unknown and dangerous currents. There is certainly room for a revelation from God, for correction, for instruction, and for reproof. Says Professor Bruce: "By reason of sin, the confusion of social life, and the apparent play of mechanical necessity in the events of the world, the light of intuition is dim. Our intuitions and inferences require confirmation; our faith, in its weakness, cries out for help. What we need, we get in the Gospels."

5. Intuitions may be called forth by facts. That they may lie partially dormant, waiting for that which is intended to rouse them, is certain. For are they not capacities as well as potencies? Are they not, as are all other parts of our human nature, voices waiting for fit words in which to give themselves better utterance? It is this capacity, not only for the development of the instinct in its own province as an instinct, but as a power to free itself from the oppression of other influences and to avail itself of other outside forces that it may have opportunity to work out its legitimate results, which we have just now in view. An instinctive conviction cannot be made more or less a conviction in itself; but it can be obscured and debased by other and outside potencies; and it can also be clarified and so, in its actual workings, be made of larger worth.

And just here there is room for a parallel revelation which shall present those facts, whether

Hebraistic or Christian, which tend toward rousing these intuitions to their normal energy. The idea, native to the human mind, of one God and he a spiritual being, is kept in proper exercise by having the attention directed to moral and spiritual truths. These moral and spiritual facts create a clearer atmosphere in which the intuition can best give us its deliverances. A religious education in which the mind and soul are early led to use the moral and spiritual powers, tends to liberate these instincts and give them largest room for exercise. Taught to regard God as a Spirit and one's central self as also a spirit, there is the consciousness of acting in a spiritual realm of things, the reality of which is not only assured by the parallel facts, but by the deepest and most central conviction of our very nature itself. Whatever helps us from the outside, carries with it a kind of evidence that it comes from the God whose sign-manual is set upon it. That thing which is so helpful is thus shown to be a co-partner with these instincts in the moral realm of things. It is in this way—by outside and parallel facts which minister best to these moral convictions—that we find the difference between the "pure indestructible Godward instinct" and those depraved conceptions of the idea of God which have been so baleful in human history.

6. These moral intuitions are mutually consistent. Consistency with each other is not enough to claim for them, but each is consistent with the whole. Sir William Hamilton, speaking of these primary convictions of the human soul, says:

They are many; they are in co-ordinate authority, and their testimony is clear and precise. It is therefore competent for us to view them in correlation, to compare their declarations. No attempt to show that the data of consciousness are mutually contradictory has yet succeeded.

The reason is evident. They are together what hands and feet and heart and brain are to the body—parts of one vital system. The eye is not only for the light and the air for the lungs, but all four of them are adaptations of man to the physical world and of the physical world to man. And thus it comes about that plain men, scarcely able to formulate these instincts and to separate one from the other, act upon them freely, and know only this, that they have a general conviction about religious truth which nothing can dislodge. Many a plain Christian can be thrown into a state of doubt when an opponent comes to him with purely logical difficulties. He cannot answer the objector, but he knows that the objection can be answered at some time and by somebody, because the moral instinct within him abides firm. He knows the opponent is wrong; but how he knows it, he is not able to say. So that the strong logician, who has his laugh against "the narrowness of the men who will not yield to reason," may be the narrower of the two, since he uses but one side, and that not the largest or the surest side, of himself on moral themes. The fact that these convictions are mutually consistent brings about, in such a plain man's mind, a whole inner world of exchangeable moral moods and sympathies which fortify him against such assaults. On some special lines he has not as yet accurately sounded and mapped out his own deeper selfhood. But his moral convictions have been roused by the contact with revealed truth.

And so the assaults of unbelief have been in vain. For the moral intuitions, working together, have detected the fact that something was wrong in the plausible objection. So that plain men, by the happy care which gave them as an original part of themselves this inner body of moral truth, have often been saved from error and sin when no other aid was at hand. Soon thereafter they may have refreshed their own minds by the scriptural statement of the truth. But the assault found its first resistance in their own instinctive convictions. A God who is a spiritual being is a correlative fact with a spiritual nature in man. The distinction, vital and indestructible, between "the true and the false," demands a Standard Mind, agreement with whom is the rectification of this distinction; since his conviction is the absolute truth. A moral God is for the same reason the Standard Soul of the universe, agreement with whom is "the right," and disagreement with whom is "the wrong."

This God, a moral God, is also by correlation of ideas, a Moral Governor. And by the same connection of principles, a moral governor of man must be man's final Judge, to whose decision the limited time of a probation looks forward—a decision being necessary at the close of any period of probation. There is thus the relation and the interaction of these intuitions. And such a free play of these principles used by the plain everyday men, of whom the great mass of the race is made up, is itself a notable fact in the Divine ordering of the world's moral life.

7. These intuitions are prophetic. The hands on the human body are made to grasp. They are prophetic of a world outside the hands themselves. All faculties of body and mind—unless one should claim that these moral instincts are the exception—are prophetic. But why should any one ask to have these integral parts of our nature excepted? The fact that they work differently from the rest of our mental and moral organism, is exactly paralleled by our bodily organism, in which some parts work in ways unlike others. The body does not terminate on itself; no more does the mind. They are each in a certain sphere of things to which they are correlated. The correlation is as much a fact as the organism. All this is prophetic.

In the old Hebrew religion there were prophetic rites and ceremonies. Some of that nation saw only the rite and never the meaning; only the ritual, never what it betokened; only the shadow, never the substance; only the orderly procedure of the service, never the glorious prophecy of the Messiah of God. So it is about these intuitions. Some would stop with them. But a hundred times the experiment has been tried, until it is sure that to stop with them is to stifle them. A few merely philosophical men, amusing their intellectual leisure by discussing these fundamental instincts, have proposed to accept them as a religion. But neither they themselves, nor any appreciable fraction of the human race, has ever stood on that ground for any length of time. To collect the words of dissatisfaction which the best of these men have uttered would be an easy but an unnecessary labor. Philosophy teaches about a religion, but it is not itself a religion. If you set down its value in itself alone, if you consider it as its own end, you will find that the estimate of its influence on the world at large is but inconsiderable. It is the hands grasping—but grasping at air. The feet lifted to walk—but left lifted. It is appetite without bread; it is thirst without the natural supply of water. There is a vast cumulative want. With close study men may, by the light of the intellect, look down into the soul and see and tabulate its instinctive ideas. But this is to make a philosophy rather than to discover a religion. And after the study is completed, the satisfaction is not that of the satisfied soul, but only the merely intellectual satisfaction of having discerned that the instinct is a fact of our human nature.

The religions of the world have, alike by the perversion and by the satisfaction of these moral instincts, shown that they crave a person. Whether this does or does not involve a peculiar and even inspired record of the sayings and doings, both ordinary or extraordinary, of this person, is to be afterward considered. But the first thing is the person who shall gather up, with due recognition and endorsement, these instincts. The attempts to supply this need of a person have given us heroes and demigods, lords many and manifold, who have been worshiped more or less fully by their fellow-men. The long line of mythological personages shows that the worshipful spirit, the result of these instincts, is a power among mankind. If the One Holy God has been discarded, the idea of a god of some sort remains. Reverence requires a person to be reverenced.

It is the same with the other perversions of original moral intuitions. The singular applications of the idea of God's care as extending only to a class of things or to a class of men; the singular limitations of the idea of the right and the wrong, so that kingly or priestly men were exempted from the law that binds others; the singularly grotesque conceptions of the immortal life in its heaven and its hell; the strangely fantastic ideas connected with the final day of judgment—all these things show that, in such a world as ours and in such a race as this of which we are members, there is need of rectification from without by some one who can clear away the *débris* of the fall and restore man to his primitive selfhood. These primary convictions were primarily trustworthy. They are sure when we get back to them in their original force and purity. And the book that can reassert, confirm, and enforce them must also be a sure and trustworthy book, with all of inspiration which such a book involves.

In another way, the degree of success gained by religions has shown the same fact. A person is to emerge in all the older and better beliefs. They all have a version, varied somewhat, of the primal promise, that One should appear to bruise the evil one who had so bruised and taken captive the race.

In naming these primitive ideas in the human mind in the earlier part of this chapter, the profound expectation of a person as the world's teacher and deliverer and saviour was not included. And the omission was less because of doubt concerning it, and more because it will be conceded by all that there is at least an aptitude for it. There is a preparation, a presumption. It stands very near to a first truth. It is close upon a primary conviction. There is an appetency for it. All the grand old historic souls of the world got from their own or from succeeding generations a little fragment of the reverence and worship that, in its fullness, can be given only to some divine Person who assembles in himself all the separate excellences they had exhibited, and who naturally demands therefore the utmost of reverence and devotion. This idea, indestructible when once proclaimed, universally received when once announced, exactly fits all these primitive instincts, even if it is not itself one of them.

But the men who are appointed to represent each in some faint degree the excellences of this expected One must be in a series, and over them must preside a divine Providence. God's guidance of things and men, his intervening hand through law, or, if need ever be, above law, is the inspiration of all history. That the events are inspired in the sense that they are guided toward the world's readiness to apprehend the Person who is to restore the race, is one of the main things about inspiration. It is the inspiration not only of single events, but it is inspiration in marshaling them in an orderly series. The chain, link by link, is forged and united. No link is too small for the care of the One who constructs it all out of the freedom of all things and all men under his laws. The inspiration of the events is that out of which all other kinds of inspiration can come. Other inspiration demanded is supplementary. The events bring in due time the Person. The Bible is the record of the series of these inspired occurrences, of the evolution of them with reference to the Person, and of their culmination in the person and work of Christ Jesus.

It will be admitted that these primary truths, described in the earlier part of this chapter, are taken up, endorsed, and employed in the Bible. As these "moral axioms" agree among themselves, so they agree with this book. The New Testament does not traverse any one of them. It clarifies them. It newly applies them. Its Christ ever appeals to them. Its apostles simply expand his utterances. The authority of the apostles is not original, but derived from him. They also work on the same basis of these instinctive convictions.

It is true that the Bible takes into account, as these primitive cognitions do not, certain damaging facts resulting from human sin. But in estimating this disturbance from normal conditions, one source of its appeal is to this indestructible sense of the right and wrong in us. By this instinctive moral standard we know of the sin and so of the need of the forgiveness and restoration. The book clears away the mists that rise from this sinning nature. The book sharpens to its original potency the sense of God as holy, of him as the moral governor of the world, and of him as the one we must meet in judgment, and with whom we must abide or from whom we must depart forever. Of the remedy for sin's dominion and doom these instincts say nothing. They only help us to judge of the extent of the need. They prepare us for that widespread expectation of a Divine Person who is the world's hope. But just because they cannot tell us more definitely, they hold out welcoming hands toward the book which records for us what we know of the Person. The book thus comes to stand very close to these fundamental truths involved in all our thought on moral themes. All their trend is toward it. They are mutual agents in a common realm of things. The primitive convictions of the moral nature and of the book are so nearly one—the book indeed going farther, but always along the same lines as they—that for a vast number of plain men the authority of the one is practically that of the other. The testimony from the two sources of authority is so mingled in their minds that the difference between the inner and outer handwritings is not really distinguished. The book is about a person. Christianity is differentiated from all other religions in that it gathers, not primarily about precepts or even doctrines, but about a person, Jesus Christ. Each Christian is a person also, with a personality capable of being moved in its central depths by this Person. Mahomet was not Islam, but only its prophet. Christ himself is Christianity. For this good reason the Bible, which has for its center this Christ, takes hold of these primary convictions. The book with its Christ and the handwriting within the soul are in close conformity. They live and breathe and glow and throb as one. They find the same goal. To multitudes the apprehension of the person revealed in the book rectifies, strengthens, persuades, dominates the conscience within their own souls. The purest consciousness is that of men who have an experience of the religion of Jesus Christ. We can study with best results these Christian souls in which there is a consciousness most nearly normal. We get nearest the true manhood of man in such men. And invariably they are men saturated with this book. They have the Holy Spirit witnessing in their spirits that they are the children of God.

Some things the common consciousness of the human race gives us. Some things are given us by the special consciousness of the great consenting religious experience of Christians. Experimental religion has its deliverances about the book, about the person in whom it centers, and about the agreement of the person and of the book with the affirmations of our clearest and most exalted moral moods. In the great consensus of Christian experience we get testimony in its purest form. The Lick Observatory, with its larger disk and longer range and greater height and clearer atmosphere, gets itself accepted in its discoveries by the whole astronomic world. Farther on, we shall study more largely this religious experience to find its contents and its deliverences. But, here and now, it is quoted as a parallel fact with those other utterances and is, with them, closely allied to a whole series of consenting and agreeing moral facts. The book and these primitive convictions give us just that alliance which broadens the moral basis for our induction. We are gathering a vast amount of moral material which, by its certainty and positiveness, is of great worth on the question of inspiration.

In the examination of our primary moral intuitions we saw certain facts which are a warrant for conclusions. Close to them, in especial agreement with them and tending to free these convictions from obscurity and to give them larger scope, we saw that a certain book, popularly called the Bible, is of great value.

Section II.
Our Actual Bible

Its endorsement of these convictions, its statements concerning certain great facts, and the experience which it has generated in the human soul, are parallel phenomena. Multitudes of plain men never make the distinction between the primary truths learned by analysis of their own natural convictions and those which are engendered by the teachings of the Bible. It must be, for them, the Bible as a standard of appeal. They are so situated in life, so constituted mentally and morally, so unpractised in intricate reasoning from distinctly discovered "moral axioms" and "primary truths," that the basis of moral appeal for them is the Bible. This is not due to their ignorance. For in lines of commercial and political life they are not ignorant. But they are busy men, in a busy world, who elsewhere do not work from primary commercial and political principles distinctly recognized and avowed. They gain their commercial and political education in other and outside ways. They feel the power of trend, and use it along the lines of their life. The man at the wheel steers the ship; but he does it through the knowledge of navigation which the master mariner possesses. The master of the ship tells the helmsman the course he is to steer. This sailor has little knowledge at first hand of astronomy or of navigation; but he can recognize the captain's competency in these things. It is in part knowledge and in part trust. He knows enough to trust for what he does not know. It must be so with the great mass of mankind. We are all made to trust, and there is that which we are to trust. The book stands so exactly related to these primary instincts, is so manifestly their fulfillment as prophecy, their complement as the half-sphere demands the whole, that we can now look at certain basal facts of the book itself.

I. The book is clearly a growth. It has then the token of life. The difference between a thing dead and a thing living is that one increases and the other grows. The stone gains from without; but the plant gains by growing from within outward. Its long finger-like roots are endowed with the power of search for what it can take in and use for building itself up. It rejects that which is harmful and useless. It finds the right drop of moisture for its thirst, and the fit morsel of soil for its food. It responds to sunshine and rain. It is alive. The life glows as well as grows. It thrusts out fitting branch and leaf and fruit. It utilizes all things that it can reach in its growth. The Bible is no stone increasing by outside and unsympathetic additions. It puts on its parts upon the principle of growth. It vitalizes the material it uses. It has an inward and mysterious principle of life. It grew. It did not happen. It was not ready-made in the skies and "let down as so many golden plates," after the crass conception ascribed to the Mormon Bible. It is at the exact opposite of all that. It is the one great original instance of a true evolution. And while star-eyed science has been looking ever since its birth for some simple principle which should unify with the power of true life all this wide universe of things and has clapped its hands in almost infantile glee over the newly discerned idea of evolution, it has only recognized what, under other names, was claimed twenty centuries ago for the Hebrew Scriptures, and what Christian commentaries have from the first declared, that the Bible from its Genesis to its Revelation shows evolutionary progress. It is the foremost instance of a divine thought evolved, developed, and embodied in shapely form. The whole idea of the book is unique. It gives us a series of inspired events, some of them natural,— and none the less inspired because natural,—some of them supernatural. They grew under God's touch and were recorded under the same shaping and guiding hand. Men are acting freely in these events, but God at the same time is inspiring the events; men are acting freely in recording the inspired events, but God is as free to use their freedom, so as to make the record trustworthy. This is the living fact about this living book. It possesses itself—so thoroughly alive is it—of all forms of literature, to inspire them with its vital idea. It appropriates them all, and builds itself up by them all; just as does the plant that selects its own drop of water and bit of soil. Using thus all varieties of literary form, it gets its various hold on men of all aptitudes. It has its scraps of history as old perhaps as Abraham—it may be older; and these are woven together by Moses, and then touched and retouched, it may be, until their final form under Ezra. It has biographical sketches, moral etchings, elaborately wrought pictures of men long since dead; but their history is so strikingly instructive that they rule us still from their silent urns. The book has its songs by Hebrew bards; and they are more frequently quoted than those of the Grecian Homer or the English Shakespeare. It has its prophecies; and their fulfillment is the marvel of every man who sees a Hebrew face on the street of any city upon any continent of the world. It has its Gospels, the vividness of which makes one almost see their Christ, the artlessness of the writers snatching a grace beyond the reach of art. It has its brotherly letters—epistles we call them, though letters were a better name—letters that discuss the grandest doctrines and yet are so familiar that they talk about a cloak at Troas and tell a woman at Corinth to wear her hair so as to suggest no immodesty. There are men so logically and judicially constructed in mind as to demand the authority of miracles as the basis of belief in a revelation from God; and here they find their miracles. Others are charmed and held and blessed by parabolic teaching; and here it is given them. For those who crave clearly stated doctrines with no needless word added and no necessary word omitted, there are doctrinal discussions. For those who crave emotion in religion there are the "lively oracles" about the death and the resurrection of the Lord. There are those who want direction for the life that now is; and this book sets it before them, while at the same time it tells them of the life everlasting. It is a living book for living men.

Some persons want to put it down upon a dissecting table and cut and carve it. But that can only be done to a corpse. You may not try that method with your friend when he offers you his hand. You grasp his in return. This book meets you with a generous grasp. Its flexibility of form, its non-scientific method, its simple carelessness about apparent contradictions show that it is friendly for friends. It is a book of confidences for those who will confide in it. It trusts and calls for trust. It has such a plain, simple, and straightforward air, that when men come to it with their scientific methods, with their narrow specialties, they are quite likely to mistake its meaning—much as a poet would miss the meaning of a mathematical problem, or a mathematician miss the meaning of a poem. It is the most baffling book for the specialist in any line, even of ecclesiastical learning; but the best book for an all-around religious man. It is a book for cloister and palace. It is plainly a common book for mankind. The world is filled with good, fair, honest, workday people, with men of average mental and moral ability; and the book is one which carries with it its own proof for the world's toilers. For like the sun, the best evidence for it is to stand out in its radiance and feel its warmth. Right through the book runs one living, unifying purpose that makes itself seen and felt. History, Prophecy, Biography, Gospel, Acts, Epistle, have that kind of common human interest in them which captivates the popular heart. The book is for universal man.

It is a book of live issues. True, its Genesis is about men and things long gone by. But for that very reason some minds crave its instruction. There is a living present interest in some very old questions. All the living interest in astronomy to-day is about God's very ancient stars in his ancient heavens. The interest in chemistry is about God's ancient laws, whereby so many parts of one element, no more, no less, chemically combine with just so many parts, no more, no less, of another element and go to form a new thing. When God puts his sign manual on a thing however old, be it star or book, the thing so stamped does not drop out of human interest. The "living issues" are not those of social reform, or political preference. They touch individual souls. The limits of any reform are found in the number of individuals whose hearts are reached and lifted, and who have lifting power on the community. Mount Washington on its broad shoulders lifts the whole presidential range of the White Hills of New Hamp-

THE GATHERED MATERIAL

shire. The living questions, the vital issues of freedom were met by our Lord when the civil reformers of Judea wanted him to take up their "burning question of civil liberty," and he bade them remember that true freedom was personal, was a matter of the soul, and was secured through discipleship. Striking deeper, rising higher, and spreading wider than any local question is the great question of sin and its Deliverer. This is the thought which throbs through this book, from the primal promise following hard after the primal sin to the second advent of the victorious Lord as he comes to add the "amen" to the completed ages of redemption.

II. The method of the book is historical: a method having clearly its excellences and its defects. The defects, however, are such as can be remedied for the thoughtful reader. He has only to recall two simple facts. One of them is that there is to be a recognition of the special time in which each one of the books was written—the historical perspective. And the other is the fact of our duty in this century to bear in mind the principles and aims of the New Testament when one reads any portion of the Old Testament for devotional purposes and for instruction in righteousness.

No historic writer escapes the influence of his own age or vacates his own personality. For him to appear to do so would be suspicious. For him really to do so would be impossible. For he could not be understood in his own age if he used facts that had not been discerned or forms of speech not familiar. That such a writer is constrained and restrained by the literature of his time is certain. And the fact is a water-mark that evidences his truthfulness. He may quote a public historic document which, inexact for some purposes, is exact for his. He may use phrases current in his time, exactly as we do in our age, which will not bear a literal meaning. They may be linguistically inexact, but they are the very phrases living men were using when he wrote. If he is a historic writer, and on that account obliged to name geographical facts, he is compelled by the limitations of his time to use the current geographical knowledge. That knowledge may have been, probably was, defective. But there need be therefore no error in the religious use he makes of it. The facts, as he quotes them, are true for his purposes. If he used language founded on discoveries made only in these later centuries, the cry of fraud could be raised. The Bible writer never does that thing.

To insist that the Bible shall be geographically exact according to the science of this age, is to make it other than an inspired book of religion. And a book of perfected science in geography, geology, astronomy, and ethnology would be very largely unintelligible even to us to-day. For the last word in any science is yet to be spoken. To ask that the Bible be perfect in its Hebrew and Greek forms of literary art is to ask that it be not a human production at all. It claims to have been written by men as well as inspired by God. And on every page it shows the stamp of a special age and the peculiarities of a particular man. It has not only perspective but personality. It has a distinct local coloring and it has also a happy individualism. Literary imperfection, in so far as it exists, is absolutely consistent with moral and religious perfection. Euclid, imperfect as poetry, is perfect as geometry. Homer, allowed to be imperfect in his geography and history, at some points using large license, is yet claimed as approaching perfection in a certain line of poetic excellence.

The authors of the Bible have always the defects of their excellences, from the standpoint of literary judgment; but this impairs neither their honesty nor their credibility in their own sphere of religion. And when in any court of justice, variety in the mental endowment or linguistic attainments of witnesses testifying to a fact under oath shall be held to invalidate testimony, then the same may be charged upon these biblical witnesses. To dwell largely on the errors of a man who is testifying in court because he uses a popular but inexact phrase; to object to his testimony because his words are not cast in the best mold of human speech, would show a lawyer who knew he had a poor cause and was raising dust to obscure justice. To attempt to impugn the veracity of a man because in his testimony he speaks of the sun as "rising" or as "setting" on a given day would show not the exact jurist, but the shallow pettifogger.

And yet, though not intended to teach historic but religious truth, the side issues in the record of various national events even when incidentally named, are of a certain degree of value. And as the great aim of the book is to show how a given promise is fulfilled in the development of a certain family and afterward in a certain nation, the historical accuracy in these essential things is basal. Only we must remember that events are viewed phenomenally. The early history of the globe and of the creation of man could have had no eye-witness. The revelation of the facts afterward to men who should set them down for the world's belief may not be expressly scientific in form. The method seems to be optical, and the defects of such a method do not hinder it from being more truthful for mankind than mere scientific descriptions would be. For the defects of the purely scientific method are obvious as a medium of moral impression, and moral and religious impression by means of the facts is clearly the aim of the early historian. The phenomenal method of describing facts in nature has been held, even by the severest scientific critics, to be in some respects the more accurate. Principal Shairp, in his "Studies in Poetry and Philosophy," says that "Wordsworth's descriptions of nature are never once at fault, though his method is never once scientific." Truth is true here from its own point of view, and from that only. Professor Proctor, writing of an eclipse, speaks of the value to science of the non-scientific method, and gives as an instance the fact that his wife, who saw the phenomena optically rather than scientifically, called his attention away from the aspect he was noticing to certain other and very important and characteristic facts. He terms this "the true artistic faculty as distinguished from the scientific." This is the old Homeric method, and, as Proctor points out, it is the method of Genesis.

As with Moses in Genesis describing the origin of earthly history, so it is with John describing its consummation. In such circumstances only the optical form is possible; only the optical form is accurate; only the optical form can be of religious use throughout the long centuries for which the book will live. The shifting scenes pass before the writer's vision. He records them as he sees them. There is absolute truth for the ends he has in view.

As no living man sees the beginning so as to be able as an eye-witness to testify to the facts, so it is with the closing events of the world's history. In the Apocalypse the visions roll, like sunset clouds driven by storm winds, one upon another, until all you can say is that the west is aflame with gold and glory. By this method the grand impression is gained—perhaps no more was intended to be gained—that "the kingdoms of this world are to become the kingdom of our Lord." Through the rifts of dissolving visions, as the scenes constantly change, there are bright glimpses of the heavenly world with its golden city, where are gathered forever the children of the kingdom. The closing of the Revelation is disappointing to those who apply to this book those methods of interpretation which are suited to other portions of the sacred word. Why should we not have in the Bible one book which is intended to impress and, if you will, in some instances to overawe the mind. These visions roll on like thunder in the sky, and their use is to make men cry out, "The Lord God omnipotent reigneth." They are true to their end, and closely examined, they commend themselves as the wise methods of God. It is significant that we find the utmost of skill in dealing with a matter having the utmost of difficulty.

Besides the phenomenal, we have also to notice the biographical method in dealing with human history. The true method of historical writing has lately asserted itself. It is substantially a return to the old scriptural form of biographical narration. It looks through the eyes of a contemporary man and sees the events as he would see them. It gets the gauge of a century, and the deeds then done are seen in their own light. Our best historians to-day are biographers. On the slender thread of historic order they string the events as seen by the representative men of an age. Macaulay and Motley and Prescott have chosen the method of personal portraiture as the most natural and philosophical, as well as the most artistic and accurate. The modern is the ancient and the scriptural method of historical writing. It allows the incidental to be recorded; for an incident lets us into the heart of things. It admits the trivial detail when that detail discovers to us the tendency of an age. It seems gossipy; but so is Boswell's "Johnson," which is the first biography in English literature, not only of a man, but of the men of his time. If this sort of work seems to lack stateliness it is not lacking in heart.

And if it has the dramatic charm of the romance, it has none the less the self-evidencing tokens of genuine history. Nor is the method only biographical; it is even autobiographical. We have Moses telling us what Moses said. We have Ezra recording, with an artlessness that fascinates us, the movements alike of his heart and his hand. In the Ecclesiastes we have mental and moral autobiography: the history of a soul attracted by successive systems of philosophic thought, seduced by them each in turn, and then coming back from all these wanderings to rest in the conviction that the "end of all wisdom is to fear God and keep his commandments."

As to the Gospels of the New Testament, their word painting has always been praised. They are sketches of miracle, of teaching, which reveal Jesus Christ to us, as we could not have seen him in any other way. They are more than pictures. They are windows, crystalline in their purity, so that we look through them as at a scene transpiring just before our own eyes. And the strange thing is that in the absolute clearness of their narration we have an autobiography of the writers that does not in the least color their story. For these biographies of the writers are merely accessory to the grand personage about whom the chief interest is always seen to gather. Considered with reference to the purpose of the four Gospels, it is impossible to imagine a better method of giving the world a portraiture of Jesus Christ. There are other biographies in the Bible. But what if we are allowed to think of the biographies of the men of Scriptural renown as so many studies toward the final delineation of our Blessed Lord? What if to each of those men was assigned the exemplification of a separate grace, which was to be conveyed to some minor canvas; and this always in preparation for the one great picture which assembles all excellences, and in which each virtue there traced is here brought out in undying perfection? To Christ the series all pointed. For Christ the series was preparatory. In Christ the series culminates. The great biography has now been written. The task, impossible before—impossible alike in conception and execution—has been done. Plato's "just man" has lived, and so has been depicted. Placed in every situation, Jesus was stainless. These narratives of his life are faithfully written, so that his very words are often reported, his most familiar conversations not withheld, his private and public life alike spread out, and that too by disciples who were themselves opposites in temperament and each writing from his own impressions. These narratives are the standing miracle of all literature, even as his character whom they describe is the standing miracle of all history.

And as the form of the narrative is thus picturesque and impressive, is optical and phenomenal, it is in consonance with the facts themselves. They are literal and historical occurrences. But the miraculous cannot be scientifically, but only optically described. We can have the phenomena recorded in the case of a supernatural event precisely as in one which is only natural, and the record can be as trustworthy. For, that a given event is miraculous is simply a deduction from facts which, from an optical point of view, can be as readily recorded as any other facts. Human language, making all allowance for its frequent inexactness, can record the miraculous facts evolved in the processes of God's revelation to man.

But another of these alleged limitations, for which allowance is claimed in respect to the Old Testament especially, is the imperfect moral ideas of former ages. The Old Testament as a part of the Bible in which truth is less fully revealed, has been held, for that very reason, to be in some respects erroneous in its morality. So far as the claim has any justice, we must remember that it is our duty to read the Old Testament in the light of the New, when we read devotionally or ethically. It is our duty to throw the newer light back upon the older obscurity. That there was among the Hebrew nation great "hardness of heart" about certain moral questions is at once granted. And the civil law admitted of some civil deviation from what would have been the highest moral standard, precisely as is done in civil law to-day all over the world. But the standard for the individual man in his moral and religious duty toward God was not thus lowered. The Ten Commandments are a moral standard for the individual man still quoted to-day. Christ's summary of the moral law for Christianity is the very summary made by Moses for the Hebrew nation. But when we would read the devotional books of the Old Testament, we are permitted to read into them our Christian thought.

Much that the Psalms say of their Jehovah we may say of our Jesus; and that too by New Testament warrant.[1] The lack of the fullness of New Testament ideas in the Old Testament is not imperfection, if considered in relation to the time when the Hebrew bards sang their songs and the Hebrew prophets spoke in trumpet tones to a delinquent people.

It is true that some scholarly minds in a reactionary mood have made the most of these difficulties, obscurities, and objections. Getting as far as possible from any merely mechanical theory of the construction of the Bible, they have unconsciously magnified the limitations of the times when the successive books were written, and the human imperfections of the writers themselves. The manward side of the Bible has been all unwittingly emphasized at the expense of the Godward side. And words have been spoken about the errancy of the book which in many cases were unadvised. Reactions from traditionalism are as liable to mistake as any mere traditionalism can be. In attempting to show that some theories of inspiration are mistaken, the historic difficulties have been made to assume a prominence wholly unwarranted by a full and fair study of the facts. To insist that these things to which reference has been made are actual imperfections, to look upon them apart from their own historic setting, and therefore to speak of the errancy of the Bible, is an unwarranted and unhistoric use of words. These things

---

[1] Heb. 1 : 8.

so far from making the book untrustworthy, confirm our faith in the accuracy of the volume. They show the peculiar aroma of the age, the flavor of the period when the books were written. Thousands of scholarly men who have carefully weighed the alleged instances of discrepancy, misquotation, and mistake of any sort whatsoever, making due allowance for the facts above named, can honestly say that not one of these things seems to be a real error; nor by all of these things, is their belief in the Bible disturbed. They would unite in the comprehensive statement of Farrar: "Nor has the widest learning or acutest ingenuity of skepticism ever pointed to one complete and demonstrable error of fact or doctrine in the Old or New Testament."

But the thing to which this accuracy all ministers and in which it all culminates is the vital thought of man's redemption by the God of all grace through Jesus Christ. Schleiermacher says, "Christianity alone is the religion of redemption." It is the accuracy of its aim which becomes so conspicuous to a diligent student of the Bible. The book is a record of the genesis of the idea, of its steady development, and of its future success. If the redemptive process is not recognized the Bible is not really seen. If that process is unreal then the book is fictitious and is untrustworthy. And equally is it true that if the Bible is untrustworthy the redemptive process, so far as any knowledge we have of it, is unreal. They stand or fall together for us. It might be possible to imagine some kind of a process of human reconstruction as going on apart from anything we do really know. But a redemptive process with redemptive facts as a series culminating at Calvary, is unknown apart from the Bible.

As we found our "primitive convictions" touched by a Bible that stands next to them, so our profoundest needs as sinful men stand close to this redemption of the Scriptures. The primal promise recorded on the earliest pages of the Bible is just the acorn out of which grows the oak. The facts are strung on this golden string. "Other bibles," says Dr. Harper in the "Biblical World," "are not only without the historic spirit, but they lack above all the religio-historic spirit of the Old and New Testament Scriptures." In the Bible the earlier facts all tend toward the Abrahamic day. Nor had Abraham been the man he was had he not seen the day of the coming Christ. Every step of the development of the chosen family is toward one goal, and it is taken under the guiding providence of God. Even mistakes are overruled. There comes the same divine guidance for all the ancestral race. At length Moses is born and the law is given. A national life is created. New ideas of a peculiar redemption are constantly introduced. A moral nomenclature is established. The precision of the order is almost mathematical. The chain is unbroken. Other nations rise and fall. The ideas of other peoples drop out of existence, save as they incidentally contribute to the one ruling idea of God in connection with the chosen people.

And now—mark it carefully—the record of all

this series is unique. Not only is there a sense of God in the facts, but a sense of God in the story of them. The point of view of the Bible is as unique as is the vital thought and as is the series of facts. God's agency is everywhere seen. So far is this carried that men object to the record in our day because God is represented as doing so much in the Bible. The naturalist asks why more is not ascribed to law; the ethnologist would have more said about the natural peculiarities of the various races; the secular historian would have more said about the secondary causes. The advocate of peace wonders that God is so often presented as having to do with war, and, from this peculiar point of view, as sometimes its author. This unique way of ascribing everything to God is unknown elsewhere. God is in this book. He presides. His presence is seen equally in the event, in the point of view, and in the style of the record. It is God's book in this peculiar air and tone as is no other. The conception is of things as seen through God's eye. The things done are ascribed everywhere to him, even when other and evil agents are named as having the secondary place. The method of seeing events is equalled only by the method of recording them. The two are one in warrant and aim. The thought takes its own divine way of expression. The point of view, alike in event and narration, is the eye of God. "God saw," and "God said," and "God did," are the forms after the first verse, where we read "God created." "Thus saith the Lord" is the usual prophetic phrase. Just how far the formula, "Thus saith the Lord," covers the words that precede and succeed it, we may inquire farther on, when we come to inferences from our material so rapidly accumulating. Now and here, the facts of tone and tendency, shown in the drift of the book as well as the words themselves, are to be noted. The story is God's story when Moses and Isaiah and Daniel are speakers. This lofty outlook, this survey, as from a higher than human viewpoint, this divine way of conceiving of historic events and of telling the historic story is everywhere evident. As distinctly as words can make it, the idea comes out everywhere of what God does, and what God says, and of how God rules and overrules. God is in the book as author and finisher as in no other.

But not only is there the progress of events connected with the kingdom of God, and also the progress of the record corresponding thereto, but the redemptive process for single souls is provided for by the book. Its record of Old Testament and of New Testament facts has had a wonderfully converting power. Spiritual life in a human soul has been germinated from a single sentence, from a mere subsidiary clause in a verse of this record. Some single texts have a halo about them in Christian experience, such as the old painters were wont to throw about their heads of Jesus. This work thus begun in a human soul is powerfully forwarded by the same volume. So that we have the parallel facts of a series of vast world-wide events so dominated by God and so recorded as to exhibit the broad plan of a redeemed human nature; and then, the equally certain facts of individual redemption going on to its culmination, through a series of biblical events freshly applied by the Holy Spirit—facts for which we are indebted to the Bible. Christianity is the developed idea of redemption in Jesus Christ for a man and for mankind.

III. Then too, the relation of the New Testament to the Old is peculiar. It is less that of addition than of expansion of view. In both there is one inspiring movement.

From the shelves of an old library a student takes down an old schoolbook. Let it be a volume on geology. It shall be the well-known textbook of forty years ago, bearing this title: "Elements of Geology, by Edward Hitchcock, President of Amherst College." It was considered a most remarkable production in its day. It gathered up and expressed in happy forms the facts and their laws, as understood by the best scholars of that time. Its statements were singularly positive so far as they went, both as regards geological facts and geological doctrines. And yet that text-book reads strangely to-day. The great outlines of geology are unchanged. But a vast mass of new fact is now known, so that the outline then drawn is largely filled in by new explorers. The general theories of the old text-book are not exactly false, but they have been modified and enlarged, giving us a new science of geology. So that, as it now stands, no teacher in any American college would put that book before his students for class-room use.

It would, however, be quite possible to take that old treatise of half a century ago and to re-edit it carefully chapter by chapter, to insert here a new paragraph, to add there an explanatory footnote, and then to issue the book in new form. The book in that case would serve a double purpose. It would give the latest results of the science and be also a history of its development. For a student to use the older text apart from the new would be as absurd as it would be misleading. It would be clearly his duty to read the new editing into the old text. If the text-book of the venerable President of Amherst is wisely and modestly written, there are gaps to be filled, large spaces vacant for new facts; theories tentatively held; geologic doctrines so stated as to admit of revision. For the good man never dreamed that noonday had come for his favorite science. He intended to leave large room for those who should take up the undecided questions and carry them on to more certain conclusions.

Even if the learned author had had the prescience to know what we now know about geology he could not have written as a man would write to-day. The terms were not invented. The classifications were not made. The conceptions lacked fit words in which to express themselves. And even if that impossible thing could have been done, the strange book produced would not have been understood. Science cannot be forced; it must grow. The old text-book has indeed a value. The wise author wrote for his own time, though leaving wide spaces for those who should succeed him. And the student of to-day, instead of studying geology in the light of fifty years ago, must read the new editing into the old text. Nor would the case be in the least changed if the more modern paragraphs and the extensive footnotes were separately printed under the name of their new author and editor.

The supposition made about the text-book of geology, in a certain rough way illustrates God's plan in giving us the great text-book of religion which we call the Bible. And the method of the giver is never to be forgotten in the interpretation of the Old Testament. Except as a matter of curious interest, it is never to be studied by us apart from the newer revelation; it is never, under any circumstances, to be interpreted by us apart from the New Testament. In the revulsion from the unintelligent conception held by some good but unscholarly men, that because a revelation, it is not a growth, in the reaction against the idea of some plain Christians in former times, that the Bible was ready-made in the skies and let down upon the earth, there is great danger that the opposite extreme will be reached by some scholarly men, and that they will attempt to interpret the Old Testament solely in its own light. One animated by a merely literary curiosity may well ask what the deeds it records would mean to those who saw them, and what the words would signify to those who originally heard them. And this method of study has a remote and indirect bearing upon the interpretation of the deed or the word. But when used alone, with reference to such a book as the Bible, it is a singularly defective method. The error of ignorance which would regard the Scriptures as a Chinese picture without perspective, is equaled only by the error of the critics who would spoil the painting by scraping off the colors to analyze the paints used by the painter. Let us guard ourselves against the narrowness of unscholarly men; and equally, against the dogmatism of those who, in their specialty, forget related scholarship. Our changing human methods which, in each age, as we feel their trend, are in danger of swaying us unduly, are always to be subordinated to God's methods of interpreting the older Testament by the newer.

And because in current discussions there is a tendency in some cases to deny the principle, in other cases not to give due emphasis to the New Testament thought as always to be used in the interpretation of the thought of the Old Testament, certain things need among us a fresh consideration.

One of these things is that the Old Testament expects the New Testament as its interpreter. The Old Testament is not final. It is broader than other literatures; but it is narrower than that to which it introduces us. To deny the prophetic element in the older Scriptures is not simply to make them merely human, but it is to reduce the human in them to the lowest possible terms.

Every historical writer of any note is necessarily, in some degree and about some things, a prophet. He sets down facts with their natural tendencies. He becomes prophetic just because he is historic in his methods. It is a case in which to look back truly one must look forward wisely. To set down facts with date and place and circumstance is enough to make one an annalist but not a historian. At any one point of the past, a historian must trace the trend which made the next step of advancing history a possibility. So that to deny the prophetic element altogether, is to deny the historic. There is movement in the Old Testament. There are far-off events to which this whole creation of Hebrew literature moves. On the basis of the humanly prophetic there is engrafted the expectation of the supernaturally prophetic. That something is yet to come for man's good is the universal hope. When Plato's divine man appears the golden ages will return. The prophet who was the prophet of man, becomes the prophet of God in the divinely guided development of Israel. The inspired facts of the Old Testament and the inspired order of them demand an inspired record of both the fact and the order, and, equally, an inspired interpreter of them. The human inspiration in other ancient writings by which they live through the ages, is itself a kind of prediction that God will use divine inspiration for exhibiting these religious facts, both common and uncommon, in their divine ordering, for the instruction of men. All things in the Old Testament, even its history, look onward. They predict. They crave not only fulfillment, but its record in some worthy way. The Old Testament expects the New to supply its gaps, to explain its facts, to throw its moral light on what else were merely incident, to fill up its outlines, to enlarge its hints, to lift its national into moral history, to bring its life and immortality out into light. The Old Testament needs, claims, and expects the New as its interpreter. Coleridge has told us that no man can understand the New Testament but by the Old, nor the Old Testament but by the New.

The peculiar forms of the Old Testament literature require that it be read in the light of the New Testament. Take its Pentateuch. It gives us the history of the early world and of the early man. It is not intended as a record of the experiences in religion of these ancient worthies. It sees them in their relations to the early human society and to the development of the race as a race. It is more sociological than theological in its cast. Genesis, in its trend, becomes soon genealogical. It gives us the history of a family development; and all things are seen as related thereto. It is the story of the ancestry of the Coming Man who is to undo the doings of the first man. All else is incidental. The story of creation is given, less to instruct us in geology, and more to show us how God prepared the earth for the race of mankind, out of which race should spring the Man. The incidents of early history are held in strict abeyance to this plan. The early men of the race are named simply to show how they stand related to that which is to come in the wide scheme of things. There is a vast reserve. The author, evidently standing amid large material, omits more than he says, and holds himself with a certain severity to his great object in writing his book. It is the perfection of the historical style; and it has been copied, perhaps unconsciously, by our modern historians. The old "constitutional history" of Hallam is no longer written. In the newer style, as shown by Macaulay and Greene, biography illustrates the underlying thought of the age. And this method is the return to the method of Moses. An era is seen through the eye of its most prominent man. And, in turn, this style of picture-writing demands of the reader the sympathetic vision. Since the artist meets you only half-way, it is demanded of you that you supply what he purposely omits.

But in a book addressed to us not only from the human but from the Divine mind as well, the unassisted man will fail to meet alike the human and the divine purpose. The New Testament, as the interpreter of the Old, needs to be in our hand or we miss much of the meaning. We must not fail to see the common trend in both.

It might be thought that when we come on to Leviticus and Numbers, the law books and record books of Israel, we could study them solely in their own light. But it becomes plain that there is a reason for the minute directions in some of the institutions of the civil and the ceremonial law. Their nearest meaning was civil, to a Jew of that olden time. But is the civil worth of them the whole worth to us? Let it be conceded that the Mosaic code is the basis of the science of jurisprudence. Is this all that those laws can teach us in these Christian centuries? Let the New Testament book which we call the Epistle to the Hebrews, make answer. There we are shown that the greatest value even of the ritual books, is their Christian worth to the Christian world; shown also that the ritual books are not to be interpreted by the meaning found in them by those to whom, in historical order, they were first addressed. It is the same with the prophetic books. Doubtless the nearest fulfillment of many prophecies was that which touched the Hebrew State and the surrounding nations. But these nearest fulfillments, which also are to be recognized, by no means cover all the meaning; nor is the worth of them to those Hebrews their chief worth. That they spoke to the men of their times is true; but that they addressed other ages than their own is the broader, stronger, larger fact. It was a New Testament man, quoting an Old Testament prophet, who added, "these things were written for our learning." It is the annunciation of the trend.

The one sufficient answer to those who claim that the events recorded in Genesis "are not history in our sense of the word history, but only generically and ideally true," is the New Testament view of these Old Testament writings. Let this be noted, that the agreement of the two Testaments, when the older is seen in the light of the newer, their agreement as it is seen not only by our eyes, but through the inspired eyes of apostles and by the divine vision of the Master himself, forbids a style of criticism which vacates the Old Testament of its facts. These Old Testament facts are at one with the New Testament facts. They are the common property of both Testaments. Nor is it alone in the historical books that we meet the peculiar form of literary and spiritual work which demands the New Testament as an interpreter. The Psalms are to us virtually Christian songs, both by what we find in them and by what we rightly read into them. We have, in the first chapter of Hebrews, divine authority for reading Jesus for "Jehovah," the "Son of God" for "God" himself, in at least one Psalm. Farther on in this discussion, we may inquire how far the one instance warrants us to do the same in any other case where the similar thought of the psalmist can be better expressed in terms of New Testament usage. Those glowing songs, in which the "Mercy of the Lord" is so exalted, seem sometimes to ask us to liberate the thought from its former necessary restriction, and to solicit us to use, instead of that phrase, the name of the Christ of God who fills out the full measure of the divine mercy. In them all there is the same inspiring trend.

In the Proverbs we have the concentrated and portable wisdom of the ages. And where the author of that book transfuses them with the "godliness" which stands in the recognition of the "fear of God" and the "wisdom of God," we do ourselves harm if we do not, in turn, complete the process Solomon began, and transfuse the worldly wisdom not only with Godliness but with Christliness. For Solomon to refuse to add the saving salt of religion, as he knew it, to the gathered sayings of the earlier ages, would have been a wrong as great as for us to neglect to read them in the light that shines for us from that Christ "who is made unto us the wisdom of God."

And this method of interpreting the thought of the Old Testament by that of the New, is equally far on the one hand from the crass literalism of the early Christian centuries, and on the other from the absurd allegorizing of the Alexandrians. The character sketches of Moses are not to be reduced to mere object lessons on particular virtues; nor yet regarded as a thin covering for philosophical conclusions that, once drawn, leave little need for the facts themselves. The true method insists on the literalness of the events. It insists that the actual history be not spiritualized in any such way that the facts be evaporated on the one hand, nor yet on the other be made mere pegs on which to hang any man's theological or philosophical conceits. We plead for the interpretation of thought by thought. We insist that precisely the same thought and purpose were in the divine mind in giving the Old Testament as in giving the New; that the New Testament thought was throbbing for expression in the Old; and that it was uttering itself as far as the nature and purpose of the older books and the restrictions of a historic development would permit.

And moreover we claim that God has provided for us, in these Christian centuries, some better thing than was accorded to the men of the olden time, when we come to the interpretation of our Old Testament. And while we neglect no sidelight of ancient history, no conclusions justified by philological and archæological studies, we must not forget that all else is inferior to the sunlight of the gospel, in our search for the meaning of the older Scriptures.

The Old Testament certainly contains hints and premonitions of the facts and doctrines of the New Dispensation. It starts with the assumption, common even before the Mosaic era, of a God and of a soul, each related to the other and both doing moral work on a high moral plane. The two foremost nations of the old civilization in the ante-Mosaic time both held these doctrines, as shown by historic tablets and papyri. The fact that the Mosaic documents are history, in our sense of the word history, may be denied by some Hebraists; but Assyriologists and archæologists insist that historic tablets and inscriptions, hundreds of years older than the Mosaic era, are veritable history. These ante-Mosaic authorities show that the old Assyrians and Egyptians believed in the two fundamental facts of an eternal God and an immortal soul. The trend of belief now is toward the recognition of an original monotheism; toward a belief that subsequently there was an introduction of local deities, and that the older was the purer faith.

In such an atmosphere, Hebrew thought, always nimble among moral ideas, would be especially active on these themes. The Israelites, if they had not brought these ideas with them when they came down to Egypt, must have carried them away when they left that land. They were the commonest of ideas in the monarchy on the Nile. It was impossible for Moses, however vigorously he should hold himself to his historic purpose, not to give any hint or premonition of this universal belief of the civilization of his age. All words of his that bear on this subject are to be allowed, under these circumstances, their utmost weight; and interpretation is to make the most rather than the least of any incidental turns of expression, is always to favor the broader rather than the narrower meaning. Something more than the mere outlines of natural religion are to be expected from Moses, writing in such surroundings and among a people bred amid such beliefs. Shall we then be surprised that Moses represents man as mentally and morally perfect at the outset, with all which such a presentation carries with it? We must not think of Adam as an overgrown boy, laboriously gaining religious knowledge as do our children. He was created in "righteousness and true holiness," *i. e.*, in holy knowledge of the truth. This must have covered vastly more than the knowledge of what is popularly called natural religion or natural theology. He must have had not only the knowledge of sin but of redemption according to the primal promise. Only a part of this religious revelation made to Adam needed to be noticed in a historic book like Genesis. And we have the right to infer that the knowledge in which God created man, mentioned by Paul (Col. 3 : 10) as the typical fact of the renewing of regeneration, involved vastly more than is actually recorded. This knowledge comes out naturally in the statements concerning Enoch, the seventh son, who would be expected, according to ancient ideas, to be the inheritor alike of Adam's genius for religion and of Adam's positive religious teaching. And Enoch, with a glance at the impending deluge, looks forward to the coming of the Lord as the Judge with his saints, who is to "execute judgment upon all." He thus sees in grand outline the Christian dispensation, even as Abraham afterward saw a special event in it; the day of Christ's earthly glory. Bengel's comprehensive note is: "The first coming of Christ was foretold to Adam, the second to Enoch. Enoch looked forward beyond the deluge. For he speaks respecting all men and not to the antediluvians only. It is the earliest prophecy concerning the coming of the Judge." When Enoch is translated, the act becomes not only a palpable proof of immortality, but an endorsement of his elemental Christian teaching. The light thus flecks the morning dawn and touches soon the great mountain tops, as these men receive it and reflect it upon successive generations. The light shines onward from Adam and Enoch to the time of Noah, "preacher of righteousness." It shines on still from the ark on Ararat, type of salvation in all centuries, to Sinai; and from Sinai on to the end of the wandering, when Joshua was visited by the "Captain of the Lord's host"—a startling theophany.

When the national history begins in Palestine, the public record may say little of the personal religious belief of the new actors on the scene, for that is not the purpose of the records. But from many a turn of the sentence in "Kings" and "Chronicles" you may see what is everywhere assumed. The whole long history of Israel is set to this one musical idea. Beginning with the organ tone of Moses' ninetieth Psalm, tremulous with the harp-strings of David, and continued in the passionate strains of Canticles and the great trumpet peals of the post-exilic psalmists and prophets, we hear the grand chorus as it grows stronger and stronger, unto the full hallelujah of rapt expectancy and holy fulfillment.

It is generally thought that the subject of the future life is left in a very vague and unsatisfactory state by the writers of the Old Testament. But men will always differ on the question of what should be expected on this subject from men in their position, writing with their purposes, and compelled by their place in a progressive scheme of revelation, to give only hints and intimations which subsequent writers were to enlarge and enrich. It is not easy to put one's self in their place, and to estimate just how far there should be concealment and how far revelation. Persons with little power of historic perspective complain greatly of this supposed lack, and wonder not a little, that while all the great nations of antiquity had so much to say about the future life, the Hebrews had so little. Perhaps the trouble is in the vision of the beholder. He may not be able to shade his eyes from our superabounding light sufficiently to form a correct estimate of their position. But some students of the Old Testament do not so feel. And they think that as much prominence is given to the subject of the future life as, under the circumstances, could be expected.

They name the frequent references to Sheol. They are not willing that the words "gathered to his people" should refer only to bodily burial. They take Job's confession to be, not indeed a full proof-text of the resurrection, but an expression of confidence that, in another world, if not in this, God will vindicate him, thus assuming rather than declaring the future life—a method of proof even stronger under certain circumstances than more positive declarations. They cite the sixteenth Psalm in which there is the same confident assumption of "rest in hope," in any world. Stronger still is the seventy-third Psalm—a psalm which expects to see the glory in the heavens where God abides. They cite the thirty-second, the forty-sixth, and the ninety-first Psalms as impossible utterances for one who does not believe in a future state. They cite also the four distinct utterances in the prophetic books about the resurrection. And the fact that two of them, Hosea 6 and Ezek. 37, are used allegorically of the nation, is among the best proofs that all men knew and believed in the doctrine of a bodily resurrection, from which such graphic figures were derived; while Isaiah's direct declarations, " Thy dead shall live ; my dead body shall rise," would seem to leave nothing wanting as to Hebrew belief (Isa. 26 : 19). The poetic form is thought by some to be stronger than any prose statement, as a proof of the universal acceptance of the resurrection idea among the Hebrews.

But even if these utterances are not given their full weight, and if it be claimed that, taken alone, they do not satisfy, this is certain, that they mean something; that they are contributions toward an end. Nor are they ever to be taken alone. The doctrine of another life in the Old Testament expects the larger unfoldings of the new dispensation. From that other life is to come the Christ. When he comes, it is fit that the shadows shall flee, that the hope shall be changed to fruition. Meantime hints and premonitions must do their work. The Messianic revelation is that for which all else waits. "Life and immortality are brought to light" in him. Beautiful is the figure and strong is the thought. Life and immortality are a treasure hidden in the recesses of some deep, dark cave. These are jewels that only a few explorers have found. These few explorers never saw the gems except by dim torchlight. Men have come to believe that, in this cavern, these gems abide the finding. At some time they will be seized upon and all will see them. Jesus Christ has gone within. He has explored the cavern. He has brought out the jewels which were believed to be there, and he has held them up in the sunlight for all men to see. "He hath brought life and immortality to light in the gospel."

We may also look back a moment to the time when the redeeming idea began to exhibit itself. It was at the hour of the primal promise, "the protevangelium, or the First Gospel," as Conant calls it. But this earliest promise is only the seed of things. It gets itself enlarged. As full a gospel as we should expect at its time, it grows in force and breadth. The successive writers of the Old Testament continually read into the primal promise their better meanings. In their use of this primal promise, they instruct us how to use our better gospel light. They read into it constantly from their own broader views, as they come on in the world's history. And so they authorize us to deal with their deliverances as they dealt with those older than their own time. See how grandly they do this thing. They begin with the words: "The seed of the woman shall bruise the serpent's head," *i. e.*, the hurter is to be hurt by a stronger hurter, and the race delivered from the hurting. The idea broadens. At length the world is ready for the idea of redemption through a redeemer as shown in the Mosaic rites. The world waits, but the one for whom it waits is to be a prophet. At length he is to be the "Captain of our salvation," *i. e.*, a Saviour; at length he is the King; farther on he is the "Messiah"; "The Lord our righteousness"; "The Prince of peace"; "The Root and Offspring," *i. e.*, the sire and son "of David." The redemptive idea, the saving idea, is ever conspicuous; and to it all other ideas come at length to do obeisance. Each inspired man reads into the growing conception the thought of his own time; each illumines it with the light God grants to his age; each gives it vigor, breadth, beauty, and glory. It is the one redemptive thought expanded, enriched, adorned. Why should we fail to do with our New Testament light what those men did in their dimmer day—interpret the older by the newer thought, and find more and more, in that older revelation, of the truth always there, but always waiting to be discerned by the better New Testament vision.

This tendency is everywhere revealed. We see it in the inspiring thought that gives the two-fold book a single aim. And we see it as well in the very unique structure of the two Testaments as they act and interact, as they look forward and backward, as they assist each other and expound each other. There is organized thought and organized form. There is majesty in the march of the volume. God is in its every part. The inspired thought reaches even the form. You could not have a speech by Daniel Webster, even at a cattle show, that did not betray the Websterian trend. Not a sentence but has the Websterian march and manner. The statesman was everywhere manifest to those who had known his great political ideas and who could feel the power of those majestic words in which he clothed his thought. So, if larger matters may be illustrated by smaller, it is in some sense with God's ever-present thought of human redemption. It was clear in his own mind and it sought as clear expression back at the time of the primal promise as it did when in the ripe hour Christ came to our world.

But it could not be fully expressed in that age. The thought knew no change. It was just as strong in Abraham's attempted offering of Isaac, as strong in every ordained rite of the temple service. It throbbed in every psalm, and strove for fuller utterance in every prophecy. The thought is always present if we but had eyes to see it, if there were but light in which men could use their clearer

Christian vision. We ought to do it. We can indeed, when studying any historical book of the Bible as mere history, shut off for the hour the Christian light, as men in daytime descend into a well to see from its depths the stars of the upper sky. But to do that is not to interpret such a book as the Bible. That is to use it as a merely literary volume, to use it for a kind of class-room exercise in history, as one would use Macaulay or Prescott. But the divine heart-beat is the great thing in the Old Testament, and interpretation is the liberation of the divine thought from its restriction. It can be done, not by our going back behind it, but by our going on to the better expression as furnished in the gospel dispensation. The thought is there though partially veiled. It is ours to discover it and bring it from the age of the shadow into the age of the sunlight.

What is said of the Mosaic ceremonial is just as true of the Mosaic and the post-Mosaic facts, "which things were a figure of the true." The old facts needed the new facts for their complement and the old record needs the new for its interpretation. And so it is our duty to read into the older story the thoughts of the better time. The inspiring Spirit is the same in both volumes. Nearly eighty times the Holy Spirit, under the name "Spirit of the Lord" or "my Spirit" is named in the Old Testament. He is also the promised Agent to lead into all truth in the composition of the New Testament. In the Old Testament he is the Spirit of prophecy, in the New he is the Spirit of fulfillment.

The peculiar interpretations of the Old Testament given by Christ and his apostles are very significant. There are a few instances of direct quotation by word. There are more instances of quotation by fact. It is noteworthy that our Lord so quotes as to endorse incidentally those very facts about which such questionings have been made in our own century. The story of the temptation in Eden, the story of the serpent raised in the wilderness, and the story of Jonah—the three incidents most controverted—are not only named, but are struck through and through, in our Lord's discourse, with gospel thought. He uses them not as foreign illustrations, as one might quote from the incidents of Greek and Roman history, but they are for him a luminous outline gospel of the olden time, which those men he addressed should have seen and so by this vision of them should have been prepared for his gospel. The constant thought of Christ is that the Jews ought to have known these things in their moral meaning, so as to have been ready to receive him. The reproach is that they did not see the divine side of these earthly things; how then could they see the heavenly things he came to disclose? They would not read into the older part of their revelation the truths of their newer prophets. They saw only ordinary history where they should have seen religious truth. They saw bare fact where they should have seen living and inspiring revelation. Christ's whole nomenclature, as well as his mode of thought, is founded on the Old Testament.

The process is always a reading of New Tes-

THE GATHERED MATERIAL

tament ideas into Hebrew fact, the enlargement of Hebrew thought into Christian conception. Take the fall of man as given in Genesis. In twelve well-known passages Paul shows what that fact means as seen in the light of the New Testament. It is even more impossible in Paul's case than in Christ's, to understand a merely literary allusion in which the old facts serve to illustrate a truth. For while Jesus sees facts as moral truths incarnated, Paul founds arguments upon the facts. He sees in them parts of a comprehensive system of things. So that were the Old Testament story of the fall not a fact, or not one in a great series of facts, it would make Paul's arguments not merely fallacious, but puerile. It is certain that the author of the book of Hebrews reads New Testament ideas into the Old.

It may indeed be urged that he is dealing with symbols, a method of dealing warranted in interpreting the symbols of the Mosaic ritual. But the method of interpreting thought by thought, rather than the symbolic method, is also used by the writer of the Hebrews when he leaves the ritual law and comes to Hebrew history and Hebrew heroes. In such cases he also adopts the method of the other New Testament writers.

And this way of using the Bible sheds somewhat of light on the vexed question of the quotations in the New Testament from the Hebrew Scriptures. Sometimes the quotation is direct, word for word. Sometimes it would seem to be incorrect, except for a word or two in the verse quoted. But when we recall the Hebrew style of thinking, which is largely by parallelisms, somewhat of the difficulty departs. Parallels in thought, parallels in trend, parallels in related theme, are named. The argument for the Messiahship of Jesus as one who fulfills an ancient prophecy by the act of coming up out of Egypt is not one at first especially evident to Occidental minds. But the two facts of Israel's departure from Egypt and Mary's departure from Egypt with her child Jesus in her arms are exactly that kind of parallelism which an Oriental would regard as an argument in Christ's favor. Similar trends in fact show to him unity of thought. They are overlapping circles. They are a part of one series. They are links of one chain. Is then such an argument a logical fallacy? Yes; if there is no common trend of thought in the two Testaments, and if the idea of the New Testament is not there in the Old Testament waiting to be brought out in the better light. Interpret by symbol, interpret by ordinary forms of quotation, and the logic does not always appear. Interpret by thought—thought equally in both, but in one restricted in expression and longing for liberation and utterance—and the logic is of the highest order.

To this method of interpretation there is one objection. It seems at first to open the door to all fanciful interpreters. They can read into the written word any conceit that rules an unregulated mind. But this objection confounds things that differ. There are rites in the ritual law that demand the symbolical method, and the restriction of that method to these symbols is clearly demanded.

THE GATHERED MATERIAL

Imaginative men have gone through the whole Old Testament with their symbolic interpretation, to the disgust of all sober minds. The method which is now defended is exactly the opposite of that. It gives no room for lawless fancy. It uses simply the search-light of New Testament thought and so finds everywhere the rudiments of New Testament ideas. Its process is that of seeking the everywhere-present, unifying thought. It has the vital eye. It sees through connections. It finds the whole book dominated by one divine trend. It discerns Christ in all the sacred volume. Pentateuch and Prophecy, Psalm, Gospel and Epistle, are all witnesses to him. The unique book, in its growth as a revelation, in its spirit and its methods as an inspiration, is not only a book of human genius, but of heavenly origin.

CHAPTER III

THE EXPERIENTIAL ARGUMENT

Section I.
The Contents of the Christian Experience

In a former chapter the inductive method of investigation was described as one method, though by no means the only one, of investigating the subject of inspiration. We come now to that method described by Sir William Hamilton, when he says, "Experimental knowledge is given us by experience and observation and is not obtained as the result of inference or reasoning." Jovans says, "Let us investigate these instincts of the human mind by which man is led to work as if the approval of a Higher Being were the aim of life. Phenomena demand explanation. Of the scientific method, the first law is that whatever phenomenon is, is. . . We must ignore no existence whatever. Are we to record other phenomena and pass over this?" If on some day when the sun does not shine, it were required of us to prove by what we see that the sun really exists, we should turn at once to the world of nature and see what the sun has done on other days when it shone on the world. We might take some bright flower, all the hues of which are just so much concentrated sunlight; and if we could first give it sensibility and then a voice, it would tell us whence all its colors came. It would be possible to find out the fact of a sun—to discover some of its qualities, some of its potencies, some of its activities. In like manner, it is the virtue of the experimental method that it will examine spiritual results; that it proposes to see what there is in the contents of the Christian consciousness that testifies to the reality of this alleged inspiration of the Sacred Scriptures.

The experimental method in physics proceeds by tests upon physical material. The experimental method in all matters of morals proceeds by tests upon spiritual material. If God is Father, man has in the faculties of sonship that which must reflect the Father's methods in any inspiration. The one must be the counterpart of the other. The "mind of the Spirit" will be, in some measure, reproduced in the mind of the spiritual man. In the flower you can read the sun. In the natural faculty you can read something of spiritual truth. But when this natural faculty becomes illuminated by the "Spirit of God," the reading is more distinct. The spiritual man will know the things of the Spirit of God; for they are spiritually discerned. Not that the mirror is perfect. But to a certain extent and in its own way, it is a trustworthy reflector. The contents of the Christian consciousness must reflect the consciousness of God, to a degree, on any moral matter; and especially on this matter of divine inspiration. True, the mirror is far from flawless. In some cases it is sadly blurred. But if God's restoring grace shall come to any man's soul, the imperfections in part at least will be removed, and man's soul, like man's reason, will be, within its own sphere, a proper subject for our study.

We use this consciousness, also, as we use the reasoning powers which, though not perfect as instruments, are of inestimable value in this discussion. We take the method of induction, "which," says Mill, "is the operation of discovering and proving general propositions." In like manner we may use the methods of "experimental inquiry," so loudly praised by Hamilton. In any single method of studying so large a question, there are limitations. We may overstep the line of sobriety whatever our method. But guarding ourselves against these dangers as best we may, let us examine by this method some of these reflected rays of divine inspiration as they are given us in Christian consciousness.

It will be necessary that we do not regard these testimonies of experimental religion as primarily coming from man himself. There is a secondary rainbow in the sky after the shower, which depends solely on the primary bow. It comes when the primary bow comes, stays while it stays, goes when it goes. This secondary bow has no existence in itself apart from the primary bow. We are searching not for some human faculty which is a sun, but for some capacity to receive the beams of the true sun and reflect them. A candle is not necessarily lighted. It is simply capable of being set on fire and of giving out light. Jesus said of himself, "I am come a light into the world." To his disciples he said, "Ye are the light of the world."

THE EXPERIENTIAL ARGUMENT

Those men were not original lights. They were simply capable of being touched into light by himself. He is "the true light that lighteth every man that cometh into the world" who will receive him. To think of all men as inspired is to think of inspiration as the prolific source of unnumbered errors. Capacity to give light is not light itself. Besides, this light is always represented as communicated. Whatever of light from personal faculty God gives to the natural man is not to be considered here; for the inspiration of which we are inquiring is not that of man's inspiration, but that of God's inspiration. And our whole investigation is concerning the latter inspiration as bestowed upon the men who have given us the books of the Bible.

And yet the strange claim that, because of the divine immanence, all men are divinely inspired, even though not accepted, is not without its worth to us. It shows that the belief that somebody is divinely illuminated is still an article of human faith. Men believe that the light is over and above that of mere human faculty. The admission is a fair starting point for an argument. It shows that there are preparation, anticipation, and expectation of inspiration. The experimental method begins by recognizing this foregleam in the eastern sky. When to capacity for inspiration in man is added this innate expectation, the way is clear for looking about us and asking who and where are these specially inspired men. Here is a prophecy. Somewhere, not far away, must dwell the prophet. Says Fairbairn, in his "Place of

Christ in Modern Thought": "The idea of a written revelation may be said to be logically involved in the notion of a living God. Speech is natural to spirit. If God speaks it will be through a written revelation; and this does not simply mean a store-house of the best thought of the best minds." Men not distinctively religious thinkers admit the possibility of a revelation from God containing truth which otherwise could not be known. In such a case, where a revelation from God is so much needed, the possibility becomes a probability. It even advances to a warranted anticipation. And we ask instinctively, where is this book that we are authorized to expect? There is a legitimate outreach and uplift of waiting hands to receive the volume. In some material way, as well as by the direct impact of spirit on spirit, men have expected God to reveal himself. The prophet has a roll. The sayings of the book are sealed. The sign-manual of God is expected and is bestowed.

There are men who have had the inspired consciousness. That some have pretended thereto who were either deceived or deceivers is only a testimony to the breadth and strength of the innate conviction that God somehow, at some times, and in some ways, speaks to men. Just what this inspired consciousness is none of us can know since none of us have experienced it; nor do we need to know it. The nearest possible approach for us to it, is in those exalted moments when spiritual souls are given to see into the depth and glory of some passages of the divine word. It is soul meeting soul experimentally. We begin to see as Moses and David and Peter and John and Paul saw the truth they were told to give to the world. In those hours these words of the Scripture are spirit and life. They carry with them their own evidence. If there were any way of collecting all these correspondences between the word as written and the word as experienced in its unfoldings, would there be a single spiritual declaration of the Bible that remained unverified? Each spiritual soul has had a few of these revelations of spiritual insight into the inspired word.

And here comes out the remarkable fact that a very considerable part of the Bible is itself experimental. It consists of the record of the effects of truth upon the mind and conscience and heart of inspired men. You get, here and there, the inspired norm of truth as it appeared to God himself; but, more frequently, we have the reflection of this inspired norm upon the mind and heart of the writer. As, for instance, in the Ten Commandments you have God's own thought—the purest truth; and in the Psalms and Prophecies you have the experimental echo of it on the minds of the psalmists and the prophets. The record of both forms of inspiration is equally inspired. But the question always arises as to the stress to be given to each. Both are sure enough to be depended on as inspired truth. But truths are relative in importance. It is the same with inspired facts. You have the atonement on the cross—a central event in the moral universe; and you have also on record the inspired impression which the fact made upon the mind and the heart of Paul; the inspired reasonings in which he indulged in view of the fact of divine redemption. But the fact itself must always be larger than any reasonings upon it; for it has applications far wider than any reasonings can reach. And while the reasonings are as really inspired as is the fact, the inspired fact is of higher grade than any inspired reasonings about it can possibly be. So that there are ranks and ranges of inspiration in God's word. There are truths that are divine norms. The Ten Commandments are such. They are normal to all the civil and ritual institutions elsewhere and afterward established. The twentieth of Exodus gives us those "Ten Immortal Words." The subsequent chapters give us the ceremonial law. The record is just as much inspired in the one case as in the other. But how different the revelation in its contents and worth. In one, the unchanging moral law; in the other, the transient ordinance now a mere matter of human history. The teaching of Jesus about the new birth is the norm of the new gospel kingdom. But Paul's epistles addressed to the men who have experienced this new birth, show the experimental side of the same normal truth. In this case the inspiration secures the perfect record of an inspired thought generated in a human soul in view of the normal statement. And the measure of the statement is necessarily broader in the one case than in the other. But the human experience, instead of being a source of weakness, is so saturated and guided, so touched and so sanctified,—in one word, is so inspired,—that it is made a grand source of strength and a sure word of God's sending and endorsement. This experimental religion, found everywhere in the Bible, running through its history which is largely biography, as well as its didactic portions, is one reason for the hold of the book on spiritual souls. It voices their feeling. It furnishes them with the very words for their prayer and their song. It writes for them their creed. It gives wings to their hope. It endears to them the whole volume. For while the experience of a man to-day would not, all alone, verify a historic fact, such as the raising of the serpent in the wilderness, it would incline one to accept the fact as harmonious with the whole trend of a divine redemption. Not that a fact can be proved alone by feeling. But the sympathetic soul finds it more easy to believe the evidence obtained by the historic method, because of the moral meaning of the alleged fact. Through the whole Bible, fact and doctrine and experience are so thoroughly interwoven that, like the seamless robe of Jesus, separation into parts is impossible. They are one. This warp must have that woof to make up the one unique fabric.

And thus it comes about that many Christians, finding by their personal faith in some special promise of Christ that they receive special spiritual blessing, feel persuaded that this one promise is connected with the whole contents of the Scriptures. They have tested the word in the only way in which they are capable of testing it. They have not the historic knowledge to judge of evidences open to other men more fortunately situated. They have proved what they were capable of proving; and their reasoning is that these promises, involving as they do the essential facts of the biblical story, have become experimentally true. These are the evidences which to them are the most satisfactory. The spiritual reason has its place as well as the logical. The heart has its evidences as well as the head. Its processes differ, but its conclusions are as valid. It were better that the intellectual method should be used as well as the experimental. But for untold millions of men, good judges if allowed their own methods of getting at results on all moral as well as on all religious questions, this experimental method must always have large prominence. It was that proposed by Jesus himself. He says that if any man wills to do his will he shall know of the doctrine. And all these men not only admit, but earnestly claim some sort of inspiration for the Bible. They rest in it as in no other book. They quote it as the one infallible rule of faith and duty. They give it instinctively the place of an inspired volume. No man, though using the most logical processes, can afford to ignore this great spiritual fact of the experience of untold millions of the human race. To attempt to account for it by traditional belief is absurd. To trace it to education is equally so. Thousands of these men had put off all the influences of early education and lived godless lives. But they were met by the truth of the gospel, and changed in all their mode of thought and feeling. There was a power in the book that did this thing. They are certain that the book has God's seal of inspiration upon it.

And all this is true because of the underlying trend in the volume itself. Its own unity is secured by the inspiring Spirit that runs through it. The trend is one, and it is everywhere. It is found in all biography and history, all psalm and proverb, all prophecy and epistle. More distinct than the localism that betokens the special age of the writer, is the universality of the great thought that throbs and thrills. There is beginning, middle, and end. The path never turns aside. The facts never get out of their place in the series. The peculiar "making for an end" is never wanting which secures the dependence and interdependence of the single parts; each is for the other and all make for one grand goal. And so the logic of Christian inference which finds one set of facts involved in another, and which, by the vital eye, sees correlative and agreeing truth, and through sympathetic affiliation makes the Bible one book, has due warrant in this special tendency everywhere seen. It gives room for Christian confidence.

Section II. The Worth of this Experience as an Argument

It is sometimes urged that the argument for the authenticity and inspiration of the Bible which is drawn from the experience of Christians, while it may suffice for them, is without weight to those who have not this Christian consciousness. But is that so? Here is a vast mass of testimony. It is drawn from the consciousness of thousands whose testimony on any other subject would be entitled to credence. This testimony is of intellectual worth to the men who have not had the experience themselves. Thousands have not had experience in recovery from a given disease. They have not been cured by a given specific. But there is a vast mass of testimony as to the effect of aconite and of quinine and of nux vomica as drugs, and of the benefit, under certain conditions, of stimulants. Medical men, on the basis of this testimony, write learned volumes on diseases and their treatment. They accept the testimony of other men's experience. They ought to do so. Experience of others may be in some cases more valuable and trustworthy than one's own. You may be a better observer of the course of a fever in your friend than in yourself. Testimony as to experience is everywhere received and given its place as of more or less worth. Nor can all these long centuries of Christian experience be ignored by those not themselves Christians. It is nothing to the point for one to say that he has had no such experience. The negation of experience in one man counts for nothing as against the positiveness of another man's experimental knowledge in religion. But the man who has not had the experience himself is bound to give credence to the facts to which others testify. Facts of experience are as substantial facts as we know, and a man may no more set them aside than he may dismiss the facts of gravity in his study of the physical world.

It is sometimes said by way of disparagement, that this experiential consciousness is mere feeling.

THE EXPERIENTIAL ARGUMENT

It is enough reply to say that feeling is just as real a fact as the existence of a piece of granite. Feeling is one of the potencies of life. Love, that rules the world, is a feeling. It is the grandest, surest, most substantial factor in human conduct. What a man loves is the main thing about him. Love is character, bad or good. Think of a man attempting any analysis of human history in a nation or of life in a man, with no reference to the fact that love is a power that sways men profoundly. At the last analysis states of mind, such as love and hate, joy and sorrow, hope and despair, are the most certainly known of all our human knowledge. And so far from a disparagement, we claim it as one of the surest of evidences that Christian souls, thrilled with love to God, have this experimental conviction that the Bible is an inspired volume. It has been wrought in them most centrally, has been ascertained by them in the depths of their own being. And no man of a philosophical turn of mind can afford either to ignore or to neglect this vast amount of testimony. The contents of the human consciousness, when this consciousness exists in the purest form—that of Christian consciousness—cannot fail to be of immense importance to every careful student of the question of inspiration. These persons are the most competent of all men to give testimony on this matter. "He that is spiritual judgeth all things."

In questions of music we give special weight to the opinion of the musician. In questions about mathematics we consult the man of mathematical genius and attainment. We make use everywhere else of specialists. Why not give here in our investigation of the spiritual fact of inspiration an especial importance to the testimony of spiritually minded men?

The experimental method alone may not satisfy some investigators. Like the inductive method, it has its limitations and its liabilities to mistake, when it is employed exclusively. But this at least is clear, that its trend, like that of the inductive method, is unmistakable. It is a factor in the problem. Certain minds are so constituted that, in regard to the inspiration of the Bible just as in regard to the existence of God, the profound inward conviction is that on which they rely most confidently. In these minds the logic of the heart is more nimble than the logic of the head. Nor are such men necessarily the least intellectual. What mind more logical than that of Paul? When a revelation by inspiration of God was made to him on the way to Damascus, his heart yielded at once. But he must retire for three years into Arabia to adjust his intellectual convictions to his new moral feeling. His head must now become reconciled to his heart. The most logical mind of the Scriptures, he is converted through the emotions, in view of a divine intervention. The revelation of Christ to him on the way to Damascus is the first of a series of inspirations for his soul; and the successive inspirations of God's Holy Spirit are given us in his Epistles, as he speaks the words which are freely given him of God.

Multitudes of young men have been converted.

THE EXPERIENTIAL ARGUMENT

Some of them have failed to adjust the head to the heart; and so have become confused about religious fact and doctrine. They have let the certainties of individual experience stand in the background, while they have attempted to decide on the truth by mere logical processes. It is as if a man should resolutely close his eyes and seek to know all the things about him in the physical world by the sense of touch alone. Let him not ignore the use of his eyes because he has hands. God gives the various senses that we may correct and confirm the one by the other. It is unwise to refuse the testimony given us by any of them. It were better to secure everything we can from each as we use them all.

And many, converted through spiritual processes in early youth, have gone on to verify, by subsequent intellectual processes, the great convictions of a regenerated soul. Like Paul, it has taken time and thought and study and prayer and the fuller experiences of riper years. They began with only these early and scanty experiences of biblical fact and doctrine and promise. But the Bible has grown for them. They now know the book. They have weighed the difficulties, and weighed also the immense confirmations. Evidences have become more evidential. Related studies have enlarged their knowledge and strengthened their confidence in the divine inspiration of the Bible. The evidence accumulates daily with their daily study and trust. They live by faith in Christ as he is so singularly disclosed in the Gospels and Epistles. The " Spirit beareth witness " with their spirits. Other evidences they have that the book has on it the seal of the Holy Spirit. They do not disdain to receive any light which more modern studies bring to them. But for themselves this experimental method of investigation yields the most satisfaction. They know the spiritual contents of the book.

It is greatly to be regretted that so many men, scholarly in some single lines of biblical study, have unconsciously subordinated the spiritual to the intellectual method of investigation on this subject of inspiration, as well as in other and related inquiries. It is easy to sneer at men of less technical leaning; to make disparaging statements about the habit of "seeing every part of the Bible as of equal value and present-day importance." And yet there is a certain something behind even the crudest ideas of inspiration, which more learned men, in the interests of a really scholarly breadth of view, would do well to consider. The specialty of any man's learning is useful to us all. We consider his results, and compare them with other results not infrequently disagreeing and antagonistic; so that their main worth is not in their end but in their trend. The fruits of any line of modern scholarship we value; but scholarship is no modern thing. Inductive methods may have been newly formulated, but they have always been used since men began to think. Deductive methods are not exclusively ancient nor exclusively modern. And this vast mass of experimental fact, accumulating through long ages, coming to us through the devotional study of sympathetic souls who have had a singular genius for interpreting the main ideas of the Bible, ought to have a large place in the appreciation of men of technical learning. Side by side with what they call the "critical results" are to be placed those which in another way are just as critical.

And the man of technical learning in any department of biblical study has need to-day to give an especial place to these experimental results. For it is obvious that much of our modern study is on the humanistic side rather than on the spiritual side of the Bible. We are to-day inquiring concerning the near material facts. For instance, we are asking what were the near national events to which Isaiah refers, and those which awake alike the wrath and tears of Jeremiah? The tendency often is to stop with the near and local. The reaction from more devotional methods makes us put so much emphasis on geographical and historic facts, that in looking at the human side we are in danger of forgetting that the Bible is God's book. So much is human that it is hard to see how much is divine. The one exclusive point of view hinders any other in our use of this many-sided volume. The study of the book as human literature is likely to make any specialist a one-sided man. And so some men versed in more modern methods of biblical study are getting to see their need—if they would be not only scholarly but learned—of being also devout. . The verifications of the experimental method are of especial worth in counteracting the obvious danger of the technical methods of biblical study.

Much may be said, some of it wise, some of it foolish, about the redactors of certain portions of the Bible; but we must not forget who was the Redactor of the whole of it. Let us use it as a literary text-book if we will, but we must not fail to use it also as a spiritual book. And the usage of long centuries of devout men, and the fact that they have found spiritual nutriment in portions of the volume which technical learning now decides to have been mainly local and national, may well lead us to examine our processes and to correct them by the inspiring thought of those biblical authors whose broader vision saw the distant in the near at hand. It is the far-off spiritual meaning which is the chief one for us in these later ages. In this way Jesus, and after him the apostles, read their Bible. The events of Hebrew history, though long gone by, were aflame to them with spiritual meaning. They read Jewish fact in the light of Christian truth. They found gospel in the Old Testament. And so it has ever been with that long series of men who, with or without the more technical studies of the successive ages, have seen God in his word. Some one has happily said that "there is a knowledge of the Bible as a revelation about a Revelation which is itself a revelation." And this knowledge is not the exclusive possession of either the learned or the unlearned. But the scholarly man, if he would be also a learned man, must use not only the critical and the philosophical, but also the experimental method in his study of the questions about the inspiration of the Scriptures.

THE EXPERIENTIAL ARGUMENT

God's guidance, in the matter of religion, not only by the Bible but by the additional gift of his Holy Spirit, is a thing of such gladness that some have made this "inward blessing of the Spirit" to be the equal, and in some instances the superior, of the written word.

Section III. Christian Experience as a Safeguard

But from such views we are restrained by the Scriptures, and also by the better experiences of Christians themselves. Such men are thrown back upon the Bible. They find a reaction in their own spiritual life. They begin to shrink from the claim which makes their own judgment, their own feeling, and so their own words, inspired. If inspiration, in the sense in which the Scriptures are inspired, is continuous, then the inspirations, keeping pace with the growing centuries, are more than equal to those of Paul and James and John. The very statement of the proposition alarms, and few dare apply to themselves a theory which is so obvious a mistake. So that the correction of an erroneous theory is found in the unwillingness of men to apply it to their own sermons and hymns and prayers.[1] That there is an elevation of soul, that there is a quickened discernment, that there is a devoutness of feeling engendered by the Holy Spirit in the presence of his own truth in the sacred word, is not only admitted but claimed. Horton, in his "Revelation and the Bible," says: "The record of Jesus in his person, his ways, his words, is so marvelously and

---

[1] For further remarks on "Continuous Revelation" see the close of Chapter VI., where it is discussed in another connection.

uniquely divine that it has cast its glory over its recorders." But to account for the inspiration of the Gospels by noting the influence of Jesus on the natural genius of his disciples, is to tell us how human inspiration can arise, but not how divine inspiration can exist. And, similarly, Fairbairn tells us "that the inspiration of the men who read is thus as integral an element in the idea of revelation as the inspiration of the men who wrote." This is to confuse the widely different ideas which are attached, even by these writers themselves elsewhere to the word "inspiration." We may not with any accuracy, either of thought or language, confound inspiration with illumination. Philologically the words differ widely. Philosophically the conceptions are utterly unlike. Religiously they are nearly, and sometimes are quite, antagonistic. The inspiration of God's Holy Spirit is one thing. And quite another thing is the enlightenment of man's mind to see the glory of the fact or truth which God has inspired.

When, in his Yale Lectures for 1894, Mr. R. F. Horton raises the question, "Does the word of the Lord come to his servants to-day as it came to the prophets of Israel?" and when he answers it in the affirmative, is he not using a phrase by which he confounds two very unlike things? Evidently he means that the blessings that come to men from the enlightening Spirit are just the same in kind as those bestowed on biblical writers. But all the great preachers and expounders of the word shrink from making the claim for themselves. To claim that our human hymns, sermons, and prayers are inspired in the same sense and in the same way, though in a less degree, as were Isaiah's prophecies or Paul's epistles, is to do one of two things: It is to lift our human services to an immense height, or else to bring down these prophetic and gospel and epistolary writings to a level, which in strange contrast with the tone they assume, would make them absurdly presumptuous. Let us hope, in the interest of a decent reverence, the latter is not the purpose. Let us hope that the religious experiences of Christian scholars will hinder them from the former assumption.

Just here this experiential element becomes, in the end, a saving restraint. It guards against putting into practice a theory, the full consequences of which, when it is carried out, are too startling for reverent men. Even Mr. Horton shrinks from putting his own discourses in the same line as those of the inspired penmen; so much better is the inward spirit than the hasty theory. The truth is that the great multitude of eminent preachers and writers of Christendom never venture to make the claims for themselves which such a theory requires. They have never dared assert, whatever their theory of inspiration, that they were under any such immediate direction or inspiration as were the biblical prophets and apostles. They never could venture the assertion that what they said was of the same authority as the living oracles of God. One does not need argue the case that were this theory true the Christian consciousness of the nineteenth century would be more trustworthy than the Bible itself; that the unceasing inspirations of the larger number and the more largely inspired believers of to-day, would have left the New Testament behind us, as a book we had outgrown. That the New Testament is a large advance upon the Old we all admit; but this newer Testament, made up of the experiences of millions of inspired men, would be a far greater advance on the whole Bible than anything we could conceive.

But the great limitation upon excessive theory in this direction, is that Christian experience still bows itself reverently before the inspired writings. All our devotional and our homiletical use of the Bible goes on the principle that the Bible is inspired in a sense that belongs to no other book. The experimental method, if it expands the view of those whose great danger is from their literary study of the Bible, tends also to restrain the excesses of those who are dazzled by a theory that their own hearts condemn. And so no man can afford, in his inquiries about this great matter of inspiration, to overlook this inward-confirmation, this human reflection of the Divine method of teaching men. Happily it is especially satisfactory to the great mass of Christians who have not enjoyed the privileges of liberal studies. But no trained student can be honest even to his intellectual processes, who does not acknowledge the validity of this great mass of religious experience.

And, more than that. He has also himself a deep spiritual nature which he may not shrink into littleness by refusing it indulgence. The soul cries out after God. It must find his light or become bewildered in its honest efforts to escape the moral darkness that threatens us all. The vital eye is needed as well as the deft hand. The spiritual insight is more important than the clearest intellect. It is in God's light that we are to see light. The sad mistakes which some men have made whose methods have been mainly intellectual, are obvious. True breadth of view is not gained by ignoring any element in the problem of inspiration. The trend, in all our honest methods, is unmistakable. But the more distinctly we mark it in any one line, and in all related lines, the better. The rays of light from different points in the horizon lead onward to the one sun.

In the previous section the reality and the worth of Christian experience have been discussed. We found its contents to be of peculiar value in this question. Devout men, by an instinct of their own regenerate souls, have seized upon the central thought of the Bible, and so have found it to be to them an inspiration from God. They and their Bible have come into the most intimate fellowship. Its life and their inner Christian life are at one. Not only are the facts in the book related each to the other, but the book and the men who have had this Christian experience are related to each other. Their experience is its echo. This is its complement and confirmation. It is the other part of the one fact. The two things are more than parallel. They approach, for some purposes, to an identity.

**Section IV.
What is Involved
in the Christian
Experience**

This united fact cannot be ignored in studying such a question as that of inspiration. With amazing agreement, men of all Christian centuries testify on this subject. They may or may not formulate a theory of inspiration. The fact itself is what they know. Many of them are plain men. They do not care for theory. They have found a fact and there they stand. They have proved, in the deepest of experiences, that the Bible is inspired of God. They have a conviction on that matter. They now take it for granted, as they do the existence of God. It is, like the belief in him, no more to them a matter for discussion. They now assume it and find that the assumption works well; they take it for granted, as they do the integrity of their eyesight, though they have no philosophy of vision. They say "I see." That ends all for them. These are good, sound-minded men—the practical men for whom the Bible was written, and who are the best judges of it on this and some similar questions.

The scholarly Erasmus said, "I utterly dissent from those who are unwilling that the sacred Scriptures should be read by the unlearned, translated into their vulgar tongues, as though Christ had taught such subtleties that they can scarce be understood even by a few theologians." But even on the score of a broad scholarship no investigator on this and on kindred questions can afford to overlook this immense mass of ever-accumulating testimony from these most spiritual souls. They live and thrive upon it as an inspired book. They detect the sweetness as they rove over these rich pastures alive with blossoms out of which honey is made. These men are in vital sympathy with the book. They are so only because they find it an inspiration of God. Let it be granted that they are not infallible as men nor as interpreters of special texts. Let it be conceded at once that a broader knowledge of lexicons and grammars and cognate history and scholarly exegesis would be helpful to them; that they might have to dismiss here and there a proof-text. But on so vital a thing as that the substance of Scripture itself is both revealed and inspired by God, they are surely not wrong. They find that its variety responds to their various moods. This cannot be ascribed to education; for some of them had never a religious training. And out of the number are not a few who, blessed with Christian parentage and instruction, had yet turned away from parental teachings. But with the earliest experiences in religion they knew where to go. They instinctively took up this book, not curiously, but devoutly; not to reason about it, but to accept it. The new heart was the new light in which they studied the volume. If their experience was genuine, and some of them no more doubted it than their own existence, then this book was genuine. If the Spirit of God bore witness to them that they were children of God, it bore no less the witness that this Bible was inspired by the same Spirit of God which had converted their souls. These men saw all things in a new light. The book and they understood each other. They grasped intuitively, with their new spiritual natures, its main ideas. They began its study as from within. They believed in its inspiration as they believed in themselves.

Inductive reasoning must recognize these facts. It must take these into account as well as man's intuitive moral beliefs. Facts are facts. And these facts about a book, as seized upon by the purest moral convictions we ever know and as endorsed by the deepest part of our nature, are so much material which warrants us in certain deductions.

1. There is in us a sense of the moral fitness of an inspired book. Says Balfour, "We must take into view not merely premises and their conclusions, but needs and their satisfactions." To the trend in the book there must be an answering trend in spiritual souls. To a certain degree we, as spiritual men, are judges of what such a revelation should contain. We can decide whether the book in its grand outline facts, in the aim and spirit of it, in its power to come home to our wants as men and as sinners, commends itself. About many a separated incident we should not be judges; but when incidents fall into the great plan of the book, there is a sympathetic discernment which sees their moral meaning, and prepares us to receive them. We cannot infallibly decide by our Christian intuition what the Bible should contain in all its historic or doctrinal statements, in all its ethical and spiritual teachings, in all its prescribed duties or disclosed glories. For if we might decide for ourselves by our own sense of right, by our own inward convictions about each

THE EXPERIENTIAL ARGUMENT

of its statements of fact or doctrine, then we should need no Bible; then it could teach us nothing we do not already know; then our sense of what the Bible should be is superior to anything it could contain; then the Bible would be simply the record of what other good men thought, felt, and believed about divine things; then our sense of these things, as those living in a superior age, should override the beliefs of those who have gone before us. And it would also be true that God himself could not give us an inspired book telling us of what he alone knows which we should be bound to accept, since it might transcend our limited conviction of what such a book should contain.

Nevertheless this sense of the fitness of an inspired book is a fact. And we are competent judges of its worth to us as men and as sinners. It has a place, though not the foremost. Our moral sense, if it sometimes would decide incorrectly through lack of sufficient data, if its decisions would sometimes differ were all the facts and all the reasons for them known to us, is yet of immense value on this question of inspiration. And just in proportion as this consciousness is intelligently and devoutly Christian its worth increases. We certainly are able to form a fair moral judgment on this matter. We can decide upon the general trend of such a book as the Bible. We can get its comprehensive plan before our minds and hearts. We can tell whether it finds us at our greatest depths spiritually. We can judge of how it affects us to take up the book and submit ourselves to it as an inspired volume. We can judge whether or not, when the key fits exactly the intricate wards of the lock, the one was made for the other. And here the deduction of millions of devout souls is justified. Not that each man has tested every passage. The convert may, at the outset, have tested but one; but that one stands involved with a thousand others. His reasoning is that other similar and connected and dependent portions are equally an inspiration of God. Older Christians have proved other portions still; and so it comes about that a broadened experience verifies all the main promises of the Bible. But these promises stand connected with facts. They had not existed apart from the recorded events. The two are one. A fact and a doctrine are the same thing differently stated; and they both involve a principle, out of which comes a promise or a threatening; for a threatening is simply an inverted promise. And thus fact, doctrine, precept, and promise are capable of verification by Christian experience. "If any man wills to do his will, he shall know of the doctrine whether it be of God." Trend in the word finds trend in the obedient soul. Both the soul and the book are "born of the Spirit." They are mutual in their witness. Guidance responds to guidance. Because some have gone too far and placed the Spirit in their own souls above the word, or have made it the equal of the word, let us not think the less of the true testimony. Because some have erred in the other direction, and have put the Spirit, together with the word, in subjection to human reason, thus undervaluing the "Spirit which He hath given us," let us not reject the testimony of God as furnished either in the word or in the Christian soul. The "witness of the Spirit" makes men sure that they are sons of God. And by the same token they are sure of the work of the Spirit in the word. The inspiring Spirit, in giving the written word, may be doing a largely superior kind of work, but he is the same Spirit. He gave the gift of a special inspiration to some men in the olden time. Another and inferior gift may be ours, as we seek in humility to interpret the meaning, under his guidance, of the sacred oracles. But the word of God and the regenerating and sanctifying Spirit in the soul bear their witness each to the other.

2. The universal expectation of inspiration finds its satisfaction in this book. We do not of ourselves know any too much about religion. Men have prayed to be delivered from their religions in moments of disgust with them all; and they have longed for God to speak out to souls really hungry for the truth. There is a thing lacking until God speaks. There is an appetite that finds no supply until God gives bread from heaven. There is an eye made for seeing, but it has no satisfaction for its vision until it rests on some authentic revelation from God. We need a volume of "truth without any admixture of error," a final standard of appeal, a judge to end the strife. And millions have found a satisfaction alike for brain and heart in the word of God. Therein one of the most unmistakable wants of the race is met. There is a call for some final authority in religion.

INSPIRATION CONSIDERED AS A TREND

It must find satisfaction in a divinely inspired book, in this and in all coming centuries. As the final revelation of God is in him who is called the "Word"—the living Word—so the record of what he was and did and said is fittingly the written word of divine inspiration. It would be of all things most strange if God, who has used other means of teaching men, should fail of using a mode of revelation which was along the line of the expectation of mankind.

And so, in an age prolific in literature, the New Testament made its appearance. It had been preceded by oral preaching. The oral period recognized, as we see from the Acts and Epistles, the prior authority of the Old Testament Scriptures then written. It expected a written New Testament. Authentic writing was the method God had used in the case of the prophets. In the Orient, accurate memorizing of the very words of a written document is still a method of teaching. It is said that public teachers of the Koran sometimes cannot read a word of that book. But they can recite, and even teach, from a memorizing so exact that it equals the best proof-reading of to-day. In the oral telling of the Christ-story, had there been any variations the hearers would have detected them as quickly as we detect variations on the printed page. But this oral testimony needed to be put on record for succeeding generations. Matthew's Gospel has been assigned to dates varying from one to fifteen years—the time of its general acceptance of course was years afterward. John's final book, the Revelation, is assigned by some critics to A. D. 60, by some to A. D. 90. So that within the lifetime of the apostles, the New Testament was completed. By no means was the selection of the books for the sacred canon arbitrary. Fathers, churches, and councils simply said what books were commonly received. The subsequent councils have repeated these declarations, just as churches in Christendom are doing to-day. A book like the New Testament was to be expected after the oral gospels, putting into form the things generally reported and believed, part here and part there, among the disciples of the Lord. These eye-witnesses could not always live. So that the thing to be expected was that before their death the scattered incidents and teachings to which they bore testimony, would be given to the world in permanent shape. God met the desire he had implanted by such a book as our New Testament. Early it appealed to the knowledge and the conviction of the Christians then living; and each generation of believers has met and responded to the same appeal.

3. There is also a demand in us for an inspired book, when we remember the subjects on which the Bible speaks to us. If ever we are entitled to demand accuracy it is in documents dealing with such matters as these. So much depends on the exact statement, that some have been ready to own the fact of inspiration in the case of the more important truths. They admit the need of a divine inspiration in the remarkable prophecies which no unaided man could have uttered. No "natural genius for religion" can account for some of the wonderful

unfoldings at once so broad in their scope and so minute in their detail. Parts of the Scriptures, here and there, it is allowed, demand a superhuman influence or they cannot be trustworthy on these special subjects. And yet the other parts are so closely connected with these of such admitted importance that it would be very hard to discriminate. Is it not better to say that while all of the material needs divine guidance, some portions of it would seem to require a larger measure of the Spirit's presence than others? The conspicuousness of divine guidance is clear in some parts of the book; but men would widely differ as to what part needed the more careful oversight. Prophecy would compete with History in some minds, while Gospel would challenge Epistle in others, as most requiring the guiding hand of God in the record. Each man has his varying mood; so that he comes to feel that now this part and now that part of the Scriptures needs to be inspired. There is clearly the trend of demand. Just as clearly is there the parallel trend in the divine word.

4. We are warranted, also, in giving prominence to that exceeding affectionateness wherewith so many spiritual Christians regard the Scriptures. The Bible is precious beyond anything that words can express. It has entered into their deepest life. There is an indescribable tone and spirit in the book, as if one had grown into the inner meaning of many a text. There is, besides that which meets the eye, a kind of holy aroma as of some fragrant flower. In and through some glorified text there seems to be almost a contact with the

God who gave it. This experience beggars words. One must feel it to know it. All day long the text rings out its silver music. There is an atmosphere as from out the other world. There is a mount of transfiguration. The new text is old, for on it are strung other texts from far-away experiences of glorified saints. And equally the old text is new; on it is the dew of a summer morning. There comes to be a use of the sacred text that the merely verbal critics do not discern. A verse rises out of its obscurity into prominence. And just as the New Testament writers sometimes quote a great general principle as involved in a single local and historical passage, so the spiritual soul finds by quick insight a devoutness, a spirituality where others saw only the coarse husk of incidental statement. And this is because the heart is in sympathy with God in these sacred pages. The soundest dictates of reason, the clearest results of exegetical study, often agree with these deductions of men receptive of the Holy Spirit. Such do indeed snatch a glance more vital. They do indeed touch a height never else gained. They get sometimes the choice fragrance and sweetness of the honey from the flower.

Now, would it not be strange if a converted head and a converted heart were far apart? Would it not be more singular if, when the best reason and deepest moral nature were both exercised on the written word, there should be a failure of the man and the book to correspond each with the other? Let us accept the fact that God gives the word so that man may believe in it with the faith of a regenerate heart. The seed is for the soil, the soil is for the seed. The great Husbandman has not misjudged in the one or the other, nor yet in the union of both unto the given end of spiritual harvesting. "My words are spirit and life."

CHAPTER IV

THE WARRANTED DEDUCTIONS

WE have seen in the previous discussion, that the sacred Scriptures stand in close relation to the "fundamental truths" which are revealed in our deepest nature. These "primitive intuitions" about God, the right and the wrong, the probation of man, the immortality of the soul and the final account, all need, as has been shown, some outside potency of restoration so as to secure their own right working. They need to be made clearer and sharper, so that there is obviously required a superior touch from the one perfect Mind, the one perfect Soul in the universe. These intuitions we saw to be never final, but always prophetic. There is an expectation about them. They demand a person to liberate them from the sin in us which tends always to hinder and thwart them. They need in our imperfect state the touch of a power that can give them their old natural liberty; that can restore them to their original force. Trustworthy as far as they go, they are at best but rudimentary. They have no hint of helpfulness where we have done wrong; no inherent power to restore the lost polarity of the soul. Rectification these intuitions sorely need and potency they must have. They are beginnings but not endings. Their worth is what they can become when larger light and greater freedom and stronger impulse are given them.

We have seen that the Bible is in such strong accord with these "original beliefs" that, in every case, it takes them up and carries them on. There is kindred between the two; they are the inner and the outer revelation. Each appeals to the other. They work harmoniously. The intuition needs the new throb imparted by some superior soul that can corroborate and clarify them. We need some one who can rid us of the confusion to which a sinful soul in a sinful environment is liable in the very act of using these "primal truths." The mariner needs not only to have a correct compass, but to know how to use it. The "intuitions" want help so as to make themselves conspicuous enough in this busy world to demand attention from our own selves. The conscience has had its polarity disturbed and requires rearranging. The watch, an instrument for detecting time, needs to be set by standard time. So the conscience is an instrument for detecting the right, but it needs adjusting and regulating. There is room and there is demand for revealed religion to supplement our moral instincts; room and need for a new outside intervention in the interests of righteousness. And if there is a series of these interventions, then there is need for the record of them—such a record as is claimed for the Bible.

And further; we have seen in the discussion on "our written Bible," that the record of the inspired events, and of the series of them, and of their setting amid the ordinary events, shows one great divine thought expressed in various forms of literature. In and through it all there beats the heart-throb of a divine life. The men who write do so freely, each after his own fashion, each with the water-marks of his own age, each exhibiting his own personality. In these things, so far from the divine thought being hampered or hindered, there is the more conspicuous inspiration of varied human potencies. Plainly it is better that all these peculiarities of age and authorship should be used by the Holy Spirit. He claims all gifts as his own to employ at will. He is one Spirit, using each man as he finds him; so that each one's weaknesses and potencies are made contributory, though in different ways, in the perfect divine inspiration. The book has thus a unique plan among the religious books of the world. History and psalm, proverb and prophecy, Gospel and epistle, inspired by one thought, become the "living oracles," the "living word of the living God" which abideth forever. By some one of these forms of literature and sometimes by them all, it holds men in its vital grasp. Right through the book runs one appeal. It addresses now the reason and now the conscience; here the emotions and there the will. It addresses in one part the imagination, in another the taste; at one time it gives us artless narratives, at another it gives us devout prophecies. It abounds in biography. It gathers up from its best men their excellencies. Each good man contributes at least one virtue. And all these separate "studies" are assembled at length in the one great portraiture of Christ as he stands forth as the Son of man, the embodiment of all ideal manhood.

But it is as clear that he is also the only begotten Son of the Father. The whole contributing thought of the Bible leads up to him. And just as clearly as the book shows a unique personage, so it shows a unique mission which he comes to accomplish among men. The redemptive thought pervades all. He is here to restore man. He sets up a new kingdom of regenerate souls. The whole movement of things has been toward this result. As a Saviour he is the theme of all the prophets. He is the fulfillment of all restorative predictions. He is the end of the old law as a dispensation. He is the meaning of all the old divinely ordained redemptive ritual. His death and resurrection and the resulting gifts of the Holy Spirit are the culminating facts of the Bible. Everywhere through this volume run these great trends of holy thought, as lines of magnetic trend find their culmination in the poles of the earth. The trend of the record is like that of the facts. God is in the book peculiarly. It is a book alike of human and divine inspiration.

Let us ask, looking over the volume, and gathering therefrom its general character and its frequent references to the Holy Spirit, what we are warranted to expect from him as an inspiring Spirit.

Section I. What we are Warranted to Expect

The presence to some degree of the Holy Spirit must be conceded. He will be likely to use human literature as his agency and good men as his agents in providing for the world appropriate literature. If it is possible to leave to men their freedom and yet so to oversee, direct, preserve them from error and guide them into all truth about the things they write, then the deduction is warranted that select men not only can be so influenced, but will be so influenced. And further, it may be said that by this time in the world's history this Spirit has somewhere done this work. Nor is there any claimant for this to be considered seriously save this one of the Bible. If we take up the instances in which in former days this Holy Spirit has used men in revelations, we must admit the immense probability that he can give an inspired record of those former revelations. It is obvious, from the whole drift of the Scriptures, that the inspiring Spirit has always used the recognized methods of successive ages. Moses' burning bush in the wilderness might mean little now, though it was the recognized method of revelation in former days, as was also Elijah's altar-fire on Carmel. The visions young men were to see and the dreams old men were to dream in the Messiah's day under the Holy Spirit's influence are no more expected or needed as a method of revelation. But to-day human literature is the expected method when man would enlighten his fellow-man, and when God would guide those who live in these centuries. The authentic document, the attested declaration, the carefully proven fact reduced to accurate statement, is the expected method to-day.

The Holy Spirit as the divine recorder has had

in mind the growing centuries which culminated in our own. He foresaw. He began long ago. He had the testimony gathered, confirmed, recorded. All this, which we are warranted to expect such an inspiring Spirit to do through men and for men, is exactly done here in the Bible. The Sinai tables of stone, the wisest thing as all admit for that day and those circumstances, have been superseded by the written volume. He who is a Spirit and who knows the human spirit in all the hidden ways in which it can be influenced, surely would not neglect to use the instrumentality of man created in his own image when he would give us the ripest possible revelation of his will. And it is also reasonable to believe that when he directed Moses to write out certain things at one time on a table of stone, and at another to write out other things in a book, he would not desert him in obeying either command. When Jeremiah is told to speak certain words and then to write out his oral utterances in a book, would the guidance given him in the one case be denied him in the other? Thought and word are so closely related that the one must use the other, and the inspiring Spirit may be expected to use them both. From what we know of the Spirit in the record —treating now the record only as ordinary history—we are entitled to assume that God will use the thought and word of free men as far as is needed in giving to us a volume like the Bible. The immense, the overwhelming probabilities are in favor of the adoption of such a course in giving us a book of religious fact and doctrine and duty. The trend of the book itself and the corresponding trend of expectation is toward an inspiration which separates the book from all other literature.

We may also reason from what we know of the men who are thus inspired by the Holy Spirit. They are men of integrity. They give us their statement concerning what they knew; they testify directly in some instances to their own consciousness. How far should we expect them to go in claiming inspiration? How often are they to prefix or annex a statement that God speaks through them? Suppose that in some cases there is at the time no direct consciousness of guidance, and that only afterward do they or their inspired brethren declare this thing. Even were that the case in some instances, the inspiration itself would not be vitiated. So too, there were evident reasons why the proper name of Jehovah should not occur at all in a given book. And yet the book is full of Jehovah as the providential Lord. The reasons for suppression at the time of an authorship which every Hebrew then living would instantly recognize, may be abundant. A writing is none the less accurate if the author does not see fit for sufficient personal or political reasons to affix his name at the outset. Authorship not avowed in some cases for any good reason, does not hinder accuracy, as it does not harm inspiration.

And this is the more evident where, as in the

**Section II.
The Character of the Men**

case of a book constructed like our Bible, a series of succeeding inspirations endorses those which precede them. But where authorship is distinctly declared, how often is it to be reiterated? Surely it should not be expected before every sentence or every paragraph. It would be an absurd requirement which should demand that the writers affix their own names and that of their God to every statement. Perhaps as often as in the circumstances a fair criticism would require it, the testimony alike to human and divine authorship is given us. Indeed, the frequency of the iteration in some parts of the Scriptures has been the occasion of unfavorable remark. The statement about the " word of the Lord " as coming to an individual writer, and the formula, " Thus saith the Lord " in some parts of the Bible, are far too frequent to please the modern taste; exactly as is the reiteration of the human authorship in some of the New Testament Epistles. Would it be legitimate criticism to assert that the authorship of Paul is confined to the opening words of his epistles in which he asserts himself the author? Would it be an honest treatment to insist that only the next sentence after his opening assertion about authorship is entitled to be considered as the only authentic statement in the document? And we may no more demand this of a statement in the Old Testament histories and prophecies than in the New Testament Gospels and Epistles. Unless there is some plain limitation, the claim of an author is over the whole writing. John's statement, " he that saw bear record; he knoweth that he saith true, that ye might believe," must be considered as covering all his claim. So too, it is with his statement "this is the disciple that testifieth these things." A truthful man may assert but he will not always be parading his own truthfulness. There are statements elsewhere about God's being with a man and letting none of his statements fall to the ground. The commission of a prophet or an apostle was attested by his work, as *e. g.*, that of Moses and Samuel and Paul and John, by the signs and wonders wrought in God and addressed to their own generation, as their written words were addressed to all generations. In many cases declaration of authorship was needless in the age of the author. No one else in those circumstances could have written the book. In other cases, however, the declaration of authorship was explicit. But always character and the accompanying attestation were worth even more than assertion. And so it came about, as we might expect, that sometimes we have declarative words, and sometimes declarative deeds, and sometimes both. That Moses received direct divine communications is expressly asserted. He declares on one occasion his divine mission in the words, "I Am hath sent me unto you." Formulas like these are unmistakable, " The Lord said," " God said," " The word of the Lord." Isaiah uses direct words in asserting his claim. " The word of the Lord " came to Jeremiah the prophet, and to " Ezekiel, the priest "; also " the vision " to Daniel. The whole series of men known in the biblical canon as "the prophets" claim to be divinely employed. Their phrases are such as these, "The Lord gave the commandment," "Write the vision."

These men themselves understood and they made others understand that they were inspired of God. How they could have testified more explicitly to their own consciousness of this thing it is not easy to imagine. And some of these men took great pains to have their writings preserved. The writing in one case was on tables of stone, laid up in a sacred chest called the "ark"; and beside these were placed, by order of Moses, the "book of the law." Ten out of sixteen of the prophets call their communications from God "the law," or "the law of the Lord." The terms "statutes and ordinances," in an age now shown to be an age of written records, can have but one meaning. In the New Testament, Luke's claim at the outset of his Gospel, and in the *memorabilia* of his Acts, are evidence on this point. The promises, "It is not ye that speak but the Holy Ghost," and "The Holy Ghost shall teach you all things," are somewhere fulfilled. Nor is there a claimant to be seriously considered outside of the New Testament writers. The authoritative words of the council at Jerusalem are a claim direct and positive, "It seemeth good to the Holy Ghost and to us." Over and over again the divinely inspired consciousness of Paul utters itself: "Which words we speak not in the words which man's wisdom teacheth, but which the Holy Ghost teacheth."

What is asserted of written or of spoken "words" is sometimes expressed of "thoughts," and the two are frequently interchangeable, exactly as they are in all other literature. Sometimes the word is "say," sometimes "teach," sometimes "write." Occasionally, as in other literature, the word chosen of the three is selected for some special reason, but in other cases euphony only seems to determine the choice. The "chief apostle" says or writes—he uses either word—"the things I write unto you are the commandments of the Lord," and the words of Paul are echoed by Peter as he says, "the commandment of us the apostles of the Lord"; and John re-echoes the words both of Paul and Peter, as we read "this is his commandment."

Let it be noted further that inspired men in their consciousness endorse the inspiration of previously inspired men.[1] Of course they cannot themselves have the original human knowledge of their predecessors as to a given fact. Paul cannot have personal consciousness of what Moses thought. But Paul may be able to bear witness, from his own sense of the inspiring Spirit, to the inspiration of the record Moses has made. Certain books were known as the "Scriptures" in Paul's day. To these books the inspiring Spirit

---

[1] Some of the instances in which the New Testament claims the inspiration of the Old Testament are: Matt. 4 : 4–11 ; 5 : 17, 18 ; 15 : 1–14 ; Mark 7 : 1–9 ; Matt. 22 : 29–32 ; Luke 16 : 29–31 ; John 5 : 39–47 ; Matt. 12 : 1–5 ; Luke 6 : 3, 4 ; Matt. 12 : 41, 42 ; Luke 4 : 23–27 ; Matt. 21 : 15, 16 ; 22 : 41–46 ; Mark 12 : 35–37 ; Luke 24 : 44–46 ; John 10 : 32–39 ; Matt. 13 : 13–15 ; 15 : 7–9 ; 21 : 13 ; Mark 7 : 6, 7 ; Luke 4 : 17–21 ; Matt. 24 : 15 ; Mark 13 : 14 ; Matt. 9 : 13 ; 12 : 7, 39–41 ; 16 : 4 ; Luke 17 : 29–32 ; Matt. 10 : 35, 36 ; 11 : 10, etc. ; Luke 7 : 27 ; Matt. 11 : 10–12 ; Mark 9 : 11–13 ; Matt. 21 : 42, 43 ; 26 : 54–56 ; Luke 24 : 27, 44–46.

in Paul gave testimony. He said, "Every scripture inspired of God is also profitable," "Holy men spake as they were moved by the Holy Ghost." There is a fair interpretation of these declarations. Their meaning is unmistakable. They leave an absolute conviction of divine endorsement when he who speaks employs "the words the Holy Ghost teacheth." "God spake by the fathers," is the endorsement of the author of the Epistle to the Hebrews when he is comparing the Old Scripture with the new teaching of the divine Son. "The divers portions" and "the divers manners" of the record "in the prophets" as declared in "the old time" are noted in distinction from those "spoken unto us by his Son," who is "upholding all things by the word of his power"; the potent "word" of the one is compared with the more potent "word" of the other. Paul, naming facts of the olden time known only from the Mosaic books, insists that these things were "given for instruction." Quoting events which are recorded exclusively in the same Mosaic books, Paul says that "these things were written for our admonition." Citing the very words of a single prophet, he covers not only all the "prophets," but all "the Law" as well in the five great record books of the Mosaic time by his broad declaration, "For whatsoever things were written aforetime were written for our learning, that we through patience and comfort of the Scriptures might have hope."

Is it possible to cover the ground of the Old Testament inspiration more thoroughly than by such a declaration? Remember how, as an educated Hebrew, he must have used the words "the Scriptures." Remember that he hereby endorses not only the general facts of Hebrew history, but this history as "written," using twice that word "written" in the same sentence. Remember too, that he includes not only select portions commending themselves to his own sense of fitness and personal taste, but covers the whole series of events "written" by the most comprehensive word he can use—the word "whatsoever." Here is fact endorsed and the record of it endorsed through his own utterance, in which he claimed that he teaches what the Holy Ghost teaches him. He not only quotes from David, Isaiah, and Jeremiah, but he founds arguments again and again on statements of facts for which he is indebted exclusively to the Mosaic Scriptures. "The Prophets," a well-known division of the "Scriptures," are cited as authoritative on matters of fact and faith. In the opening chapters of the Epistle to the Hebrews, we have the statement that God "spake to the fathers." And Peter tells us that "holy men spake as they were moved by the Holy Ghost." The seventy-sixth and one hundred and fifth Psalms are founded on incidents in the historical books. These cross references from men who say "the Lord said" to other men who claim of their writings that "thus saith the Lord" are very strong declarations as to the inspiration both of the writers who quote and of those who are quoted; and so are double proofs of the inspiration of our sacred books.

The endorsement of our Lord is also very explicit. It seems to many strange that his words, "Moses gave you the law," should not settle the question at once of the authenticity of the Mosaic books and of their inspiration. The question of Moses' compilation from all existing materials and of the revision by subsequent writers does not come into account. All historians compile, even when they rewrite. The substantially Mosaic origin of the books is not affected by subsequent annotations by other inspired men. "Milman's Gibbon's Rome" is not the less Gibbon's own work because of additions and emendations made by Milman after Gibbon was dead. The Pentateuch is Mosaic in material and in form as well as in spirit. And our Lord's endorsement of the "Law" which, in Christ's age, was certainly the Pentateuch substantially as we now have it, should not be looked upon as in any way restricted to the sentences he may quote. He knew what the words "the law and the prophets" meant to his contemporaries. If his words of reference are to be restricted to some particular saying of Moses, he was bound as a truthful teacher to make that restriction plain when speaking on such a subject. John says, quoting the popular Jewish belief, "the law was given by Moses." It was a statement having a threefold endorsement: that of Moses, that of John speaking under the Holy Spirit's direction, and that of the uncontradicted belief of the inspired disciples of the Lord. The people also say, "We know that God spake to Moses." Our Lord quotes from the Mosaic books which are

THE WARRANTED DEDUCTIONS

ascribed by him and by all the people to Moses. He gives from the Mosaic story the incident of the uplifting of the serpent—an endorsement, in the circumstances, also of facts occurring before the recorded incident—facts which alone made the incident possible. Such quotations, sometimes direct, and such citations sometimes of a fact which is more potent than mere words could be, are very strong endorsements. For a fact may involve a series of related facts. It may illuminate an age. It may testify to a whole mass of surrounding circumstances. It may be central to a whole system of things. It may incarnate a thought.

And yet, for those more impressed by direct citation, we have our Lord's quotation from four of the five books of Moses specifically, as well as from David, Isaiah, Zechariah, and Malachi. He uses the formula, "It is written." He uses it in authoritative quotation as to matters of fact and faith. Paul quotes from the other book of Moses which our Lord had no occasion to cite.

It has been held that our Lord's citations from the books of Moses show the inspiration of only the words cited. But those who so hold fail to tell us why the particular words quoted are to be regarded as inspired and those in the portions before and after are to be regarded as not inspired. The words cited are not in themselves more important than those not named, since they are cited only to prove a point under discussion. There is no reason to doubt Christ's endorsement of the inspiration of the words before and after if there had been equal cause to quote them. His formula,

"It is written," in the circumstances, is an endorsement of books in which the words "God spake," and "God said," and "thus saith the Lord," are found as often as, under the conditions of the authorship, could be expected. Deed and word and document, quotation and repetition of quotation, would seem to leave no room for any new form of endorsement.

True some very reverent and careful students do not see this. A quarter of a century ago statements were made about the impossibility of a Mosaic authorship of the Pentateuch on two grounds, viz., the alleged lack of literary material in Palestine; and, also, the alleged non-existence of even the art of writing. These statements repeated even by Renan, set a considerable number of scholarly men at work to discover some subsequent period when the literary conditions were possible, and the Pentateuch could be made up from existing traditions. The existence of a Hebrew literature from the time of Joshua onward made it impossible to find any point where this could have been done until about the period of the Exile. There was not one shred of direct proof that it was actually done at that time. But as it was done at some time, that period was considered the most probable. Nor was it difficult when once the theory had been assumed, to find incidents that seemed to fit into the theory. But now it appears increasingly evident that the two main reasons for distrusting the Mosaic period and for thinking the period after the Exile was the better one, are both liable to formidable objection.

A Jewish author writing at the close of the Exile would never, unless all patriotic feeling were gone, have placed the Garden of Eden amid the accursed waters of the Babylonian captivity. He would not study the polytheistic documents of his hated oppressors to draw from them a story of creation and palm it off as a Hebrew document, which in that case must have been a transcript of a heathen version of the creative story. It is now seen how lacking in probability is a theory which makes a devout and patriotic Israelitish priest account for the origin of his holy Sabbath by referring it to a heathen tradition slightly changed and newly accommodated to Hebrew requirements.

But if the difficulties increase upon us with fresh study, and we feel reasonably sure that the exilic period was entirely inadequate in its surroundings to give us these moral molds of Hebrew literature, what then? We must go back again to the Mosaic age to find a place which permits the origin of such a book as the Pentateuch. Within the last few years the spade—some one has called it the "spade of God"—has shown us an extensive literary civilization in ancient Palestine; shown us also that both Hebrew and Babylonian writing existed in abundance; shown us that in Egypt and in the wilderness the Hebrew story of creation and of the ante-Mosaic incidents of history could have been compiled and written; shown us too, the peculiar Oriental flavor of these documents as peculiar to that period and that alone. But more important still is the fact of an Oriental style of historical record similarly exhibited in the cuneiform literature and in the Pentateuch. In his book "Genesis and Semitic Traditions," Dr. Davis has shown that the "scrappy style" of Genesis, about which so much has been said, is precisely that of papyrus and cylinder which all admit to be veritable history. The "beginnings again," the "view as from a different writer's standpoint," which have caused some Hebrew scholars to designate the supposed authors by letters of the alphabet, are shown to be the ancient Oriental method of historic record. Dr. Davis has shown that while the biblical method is exactly the same as the Babylonian and Assyrian and Egyptian, yet the narrative itself is that of a "Hebrew tradition independent of and earlier than all others." So that what was deemed an objection twenty-five years ago, is now regarded as a confirmation of the Mosaic authorship of these documents. And the peculiar moral as well as the unique literary flavor of the documents, adds to the immense probability of the earlier date. They show that monotheism preceded polytheism; and anthropomorphic conceptions preceded the grotesque and impossible stories of heathen gods and goddesses. The Hebrew idea is older, purer, loftier. It shows the conception of man as made in the image of God, and so God as revealed in man.

It may indeed be possible to hold to the later origin of our earlier Old Testament books, and still retain a measure of faith in their divine inspiration. Some devout men actually do so. They rightly protest against any suspicion of their lack of faith in the divine inspiration of the Pentateuch.

THE WARRANTED DEDUCTIONS

They believe the Bible to be the word of God. They see a divine movement in the facts as developed and recorded. They insist that they have a right to discuss the literary methods of the Bible, as they have of any other piece of literature. They hold that the Pentateuch, so far as its mere statement of facts is concerned, could have been inspired as well after the Exile as before.

But on the other hand, the needless waiting until the Exile to give us the story seems to many an imputation on the wisdom of God. Why pass by the age when other nations who were not God's people had a story of creation? Why let a period of special literary activity go by for an age of obscurity, before inspiring the records as God had inspired the facts? Why let a people, keen in the moral interpretation of historic events, be left without the knowledge of the origin and meaning of their Sabbath, and so be obliged to learn of a seventh day as the universal observance of primitive peoples from heathen records in Egypt or Babylonia? There might be a degree of inspiration in such a record. There might be a trend faintly discernible. But the stronger trend is surely along the line of the inspiration of such a man as Moses, in an age when writing had become advanced enough to be historic, and when there existed that peculiar literary art which could only feebly and unsuccessfully be imitated in the days of the Hebrew Exile. The few objections escaped by fixing upon the later date plunge us into larger difficulties and immensely weaken our apprehension of a divine trend in the record.

Section III.
The General Course of Development

Very noticeable also is the general course of development which shows itself on the very face of the biblical story. Take the idea of God. It starts in a happy anthropomorphism. That conception for that age is itself an inspiration. Persons who have not acquired the art of getting out of the present century in their conception of very ancient historic facts, sometimes reproach the Bible for this thing; whereas it is happily its distinguishing trait. It begins on a higher plane than any other literature. Its delightful simplicity, as it represents God walking as a man might do in the cool of the day to enjoy the quiet after the labor is over, God as holding conversation with man about what he shall eat or not eat, God as pleased or angry, God as smelling a sweet savor, God as glad or as repenting, using a mode of speech, so unlike morally to the way in which other literatures present their ancient gods, is most refreshing and instructive. The Bible begins with this likeness of God to man; and never, even in its most complete presentations of the idea of God, does it cease to use anthropomorphic conceptions. They are indeed, as befits the childhood of the race, more simple in Genesis. It is that fact which gives them their charm. Genesis in its tone as well as in its form, is a delightful antiquity. Here the childhood of the race matches the childhood of each member of it. We all begin with conceiving of God as a larger and stronger man. The conception in after years is more complete, guided as it is by the Bible. But we all begin where the Bible begins. So far is the conception from anything low or coarse that it is the very opposite of these. The simplicity of the time befits the simplicity of the idea; and both are fitly set forth in words of the most charming simplicity. Never is the dignity lost; it is the better presented by this chasteness and homeliness. This ancient severity is the exact opposite of the florid literature of the later Jewish ages.

And this primitive idea expands easily and naturally. God becomes greater. He is more than the mighty man projected. He is, as the Bible proceeds, the living One, gathering into himself the intensity of all life. He is the "I Am" God. He becomes the object of worship. He is the sole Sovereign who, as Lord, issues law. He takes on moral qualities, and is holy. He becomes the God of promise and providence. He makes choice of men to whom, in whom, and by whom, he reveals himself. With this greater fullness of God there is greater adorableness.

And presently, with this increased revelation, he is also nearer to men. Idea is added to idea. He is going to come yet closer to the race. There are yet more complete theophanies. These manifestations of God grow in character as they grow in number. He is revealing himself in every possible way that the ages, in their increasing apprehension, will permit. He is presently to become incarnate in man, "the man Christ Jesus." The movement goes steadily on from the beginning. There is inspired order. The divine idea in self-revelation is conspicuous. It is all an inspiration.

And the progress in all doctrines which are related to this doctrine of God, is also manifest. The doctrine of man as a moral being is pervaded by the same inspiration. He is described in the historical book of Genesis in his physical aspect, when the writer is enumerating the objects comprehended in the creative work. But the moral endowment is also named, as he becomes a living soul in the image of God—an intellectual and a spiritual being, as is God. That such a being, formed for companionship with God, should have started on the lowest moral plane, is repugnant to all who see the glory and beauty of Eden as reflected from the sacred page. Created holy, with all which the conception carries with it, we see him fall. But we see him worth saving. Primal promise succeeds primal sin. The hurter is to be hurt himself, and the one hurt is to be rescued from the clutch of the evil one. All old literatures as well as all modern religions have to account in some way for sin. But the moral element gathering about the moral fact, which must also have physical expression, stands up and out and apart in the biblical story. Genesis is not a mere historic reply to the curious questions pressing all ancient literatures for an answer. It is a moral presentation of truth incarnated in physical fact. It shows the love of God with reference to righteousness, and equally the greatness of man to be able to bring about an evil so disastrous as sin. The mingled grandeur and guilt of man stand forth.

And then begins the idea of human restoration

which is to be elaborated through all history. And the whole idea of securing this rescue through a family which in the fullness of time is to produce "the Man," discloses the divine trend. Every step from the Genesis through the whole history of Israel is the onward march of a divine thought. True, God controls all history, and every nation contributes its quota, often unconsciously and unwillingly, to his vast plan. But there is that in this Hebrew history which has a specially distinct purpose; a peculiarly divine ordering; a definite direction; an unfolding by all ordinary and all supernatural events, which makes each step equally a new fulfillment and a new prophecy. The events have guidance. The series of men have guidance. There is a purpose and a spirit in all of the history that is unique. The things are controlled as is also the story of them. The tone of the two exactly harmonizes. He who guided the event guided the record. They live and breathe and have their being together. The Pentateuchal sobriety, the monotheism everywhere shown in contrast with the polytheism that dominates all other religions, the documents, their literary form in accord with those of their age, and yet so widely unlike them in their entire scope and spirit and purpose—these are all the fit introduction to the subsequent books of the national history. And these succeeding books never once fall below the high key on which the whole divine song has been pitched.

The book of Judges shows how the leading personages of the Hebrew religion defended not only their land but their faith, in that rude and stirring time. Its idea is not chronology. It is evidently a compilation. It has its incidents which throw more light on its times than mere chronicles could do. The moral ideas of sin with its penalties, of repentance with its reformations, of deliverances which foretell some far-off Deliverer, these make up a book which is so unlike the expected *memorabilia* of such a period, that it has been called "a philosophy of history with its abounding illustrations." The trend is definite, and is even stronger than in the Pentateuch. Deborah's song has had equal recognition for its poetry and its religion. It is a sacred war-song. It throbs with moral purpose. God's plan for the nation and his unslumbering providence for his Israel, are the sustained harmonies which befit a book that follows the Hexateuch.

Samuel, by whomsoever written, does not decline from the high plane. It brings in the work and word of a "prophet of the Lord." It introduces more distinctly the moral purpose to which all incidents and personages contribute. The splendid period of the monarchy with its promise of an unending reign of David's successors—which can have no other than a spiritual fulfillment—lifts the moral idea as illustrated by the historical fact into such prominence that there is almost universal recognition from this time forth of the high, ethical, religious, and even spiritual truth which the writers exhibit. What shall be said of the "prophets," except this, that they combine with their immediate and local reference a constant outlook to the great spiritual facts that are farther on. Oriental in form, they are universal in spirit. Seeing perhaps always something near at hand, they are illuminated by the constant vision of things yet to come. The temporal is of worth because the light of the eternal rests upon it. The prophet sees in one glance the temporal and the spiritual. The vital eye sees the everlasting truth in the local incident. The principle shines through the fact. God and man, and the eternal principles which make up their moral relation, appear and reappear. Time is seldom an element. Events are related in character rather than in historical order. Sorrows center in the sorrowing Christ. Calamities look forward to final doom. Deliverances which are political are linked with the deliverance to be accorded when the great Deliverer shall come. All events have infinite suggestiveness. The gospel is preached beforehand in its principles, and sometimes strange flashes in the details of the life of the coming Christ surprise and startle us. Surely here, if nowhere else, one may discern the abounding proofs of a divine inspiration.

And what shall be said of the Psalms, the one great devotional book of the world? Backward they look, and forward as well. They involve the great events of the national history. They were impossible but for the previous inspiration. We do not look in these poems for direct citation from Pentateuch and historic narration. Quotation must be not that of incident, but of the emotion the incident awakens. Poetic quotation is not of the fact, but of the feeling that answers to the fact. It grasps the spirit of an occasion. It voices the public feeling of a nation as well as the inner experience of a human soul. It is quotation of the inner meaning of an event. It sets forth in its own way the atmosphere and the tone which made the historic facts a possibility. Such a form of citation is not especially convincing to some minds. But to other men, with strong sympathetic natures, who see what of fact is involved in a peculiar mood of national or personal song, this evidence is more than equal to statement. Such persons are able to put themselves back in thought and feeling among the scenes of Hebrew history. They do not ask, as some have done, for citation by word or by deed from the Pentateuch. Verbal historic quotation they would no more expect in the Psalms than in a modern English poem. They feel the breath of the old incidents. They see how impossible some of these psalms are, apart from the former history and the previously known revelation. There is a vital eye; there is a vital ear. There is a sensitiveness to the inner meaning of events as expressed in song. Such men have a more convincing evidence, in the tone and temper, in the moral atmosphere and in the holy aspiration which breathes throughout the older psalms about the historicity of the Pentateuchal facts, than could be given them in any other way. And when to the backward glance there is added the prophetic onlook, the conviction of a divine inspiration grows stronger than ever. There are flashes of the gospel day. The glint is in the east.

That way comes up the sun. It flecks the morning clouds. They begin to burn and glow. Up into the heavens spring the swift rays. The edge of the sun is on the horizon.

It is worthy of notice that of all the references to the Old Testament in the New, nearly one half are from the Psalms. The vicissitudes of the individual life, its deepest sorrows and highest joys, have found their best expression through all the Christian centuries in this book. On the cross our Lord quotes from a psalm which is a sufferer's plaint; and at Pentecost, Peter, chief spokesman of the apostolic band, cites the remarkable prophecy which he finds in a resurrection psalm. About the Psalms as a whole, Robertson has happily said "that which in all ages has been the answer of the soul to God must have been inspired by the Spirit of God."

And the later books of Ezra and Nehemiah are lifted above mere annals by the pervasive thought which throbs through them. Israel returned to God's favor, Israel called again to a new and purer national and spiritual life, these are the core of the historic events. The books glow with the memories of a former time. The old facts are assumed. They alone make the new history possible. The Samaritan is found with his Pentateuch, which is substantially the Hebrew Pentateuch. The old rivalry over the Pentateuchal facts, which both not only admit but insist upon and claim as their special inheritance,—a rivalry which continues until the New Testament times,—shows not only the existence, but the inspiring thought of the former ages. No Jewish code, just then written out, would have been accepted by the Samaritans. Both hold the ancient records in reverence; "but salvation is of the Jews," who alone carry out and carry on the inspiring thought of the Pentateuch into the larger prophetic outlook which sees the "salvation" of the gospel day.

The inspiring thought of the New Testament is, in some respects, more evident than that of the Old. There is less of prophecy, but more of fulfillment. Those who rejoice to see a process in each of its growing steps, who see special design in the development of fact and of thought, will delight to trace the inspiring Spirit of God in the Old Testament; while those who care little for root and branch and leafage and bud, but rejoice in the full flowering of the plant, will see the greater proofs of divine inspiration in the New Testament Christ as portrayed in the four Gospels. They recognize in the Evangelists, the Lord the Christ; and in the Acts and Epistles, the Lord the Spirit. Seen either way, from the point of prophetic outlook or from the backward glance over the whole illuminated course, the view is that of divine events divinely ordered, and the series culminating in Christ. And such a series of revelations has its fit correlative in a record as carefully ordered as were the events themselves.

CHAPTER V

THE HUMAN AND THE DIVINE ELEMENTS

Section I. The Human Element

THE Bible, in one aspect of it, is a purely human book. It is written in human language. It is composed by members of the human race. It addresses itself to the human reason and to the human soul. It shows marks of literary work in which the writers make use of their own individuality in selecting their favorite words, in composing their special sentences, in marshaling their gathered facts, and in their whole method of reasoning upon them. Without consulting the book, just by the ring of the words, you know that certain sentences are from Paul rather than from John. And just as we say that a stanza of a poem "sounds like Milton or Pope or Tennyson," so we say that a given paragraph sounds like Isaiah or David or Peter. These men write history, compose poetry, utter discourses, and dictate letters, precisely as do other men. Their style in its excellencies and defects is matter for fit literary criticism. This prophet uses rough language and that one shows the marks of finest culture. In one writer you have pure, in the other impure, Hebrew or Greek. One writer shows large learning, while another shows its absence. One is logical, another is experiential, and a third is poetical. In the historical books the studied work of the compiler and the practised hand of a careful writer are sometimes clearly manifest. The authors are men, often of industry, for their work shows that they have compared and collated and accepted and rejected, in disposing of their material. They have consulted authorities and come to conclusions. They are sometimes eyewitnesses and sometimes they take testimony. They compose, they edit, they re-edit. They work on human lines of investigation, as Prescott and Macaulay have done. And all this painstaking work, so far from interfering with the act of the inspiring Spirit of God, is the very kind of thing we should most expect him to superintend and endorse. He is the Spirit of wisdom, and we should expect him to use wise methods.

Nor does this recognition of the obvious fact of human labor and thought and skill in the production of the book necessitate the reception of the "critical analysis" which different persons, with different results, have sought to apply to portions of the Bible. We need not confound these special claims with the broader claims of a due gathering of material from authentic sources by careful biblical writers. The attempt to sort out the material and assign various portions of it to some four or five imaginary persons, designated by letters such as "J" and "P" may be held in abeyance. Were this to be proven—as it never could be, even were it true—it should not be considered as in any way detracting from the human reliability or the divine endorsement of the history.

THE HUMAN AND THE DIVINE ELEMENTS

Most persons will ask why only three or four are named as the originals from which the authors drew their information? Why not, if we are to do this work at all, recognize dozens of these briefer narratives which supply the material for some Old Testament Luke to "set in order." The results of assigning certain portions of the Mosaic history to these few imaginary persons, are made the basis of amusing screeds. Prof. Meade, in his "Realsham" analysis of the "Epistle to the Romans," and Prof. Green, in his supposed analysis of the "Parable of the Prodigal Son," have made legitimate sport of this whole style of professed scholarship. In certain literary circles the same thing has been attempted with a chapter of Milton and a play of Shakespeare, and with similar absurd results. All this shows how any special form of scholarship can mislead and can be misled when its conjectures are not checked by related learning. The same style of apportionment has not yet been applied to the new "finds" of cuneiform inscriptions; and yet these very methods of composition are found among the Babylonian and Assyrian tablets, and are shown to be simply a literary fashion of the ante-biblical times, and so calling for no analysis at all to explain them. The method of Genesis was a method then recognized as historical. But these alleged results of critical analysis, whether they shall be found to have any real worth or are held as valueless, have done for us at least one good service. They have given fresh emphasis to the fact of a human element in the composition of the sacred Scriptures. They have made men more willing to see the traces of the successive centuries in the successive writers. They have shown how the same word comes to have a series of meanings, until they all culminate in one grand spiritual interpretation; so that the word almost, and sometimes altogether, drops the originally coarse and material meaning. The newer time fills out the word and glorifies it, as Jesus uses it in the New Testament. And all this makes the book the more thoroughly human; for we see it in the very act of growing with the growing advancement of the human race as the thought of God unfolds itself to men and in men.

To many minds this human element is at first very disquieting. They have been wont to emphasize the divine element in the Bible, not too much—that were impossible—but too exclusively. Due consideration would lead such hesitating persons to see that the divine element is all the more obvious because it so wisely employs the best human learning and wisdom and genius. Would God the Holy Spirit be more conspicuously divine in his work by employing some Israelite who had not known how to write rather than in employing the wise Moses? Surely he were a foolish man who should choose ignorance rather than wisdom in one who was to present his cause before a human tribunal. And when God comes to the world with a plea addressed to thoughtful men, he is not going to do an act that would sully his wisdom in neglecting to use a man like Moses, who is careful in historical research, broad in legal knowledge, and ripe in religious experience.

THE HUMAN AND THE DIVINE ELEMENTS

It is alleged that "to err is human," that imperfect man, using imperfect language, is liable to mistake; that the human element is necessarily an imperfect, fallible, and erroneous element. Let us look at this objection very carefully. For if this is a fact it follows that God cannot give a reliable communication of his will to man. It follows that, while man can give his thought to his fellow-man with such accuracy that life or death depends upon the communication, God cannot do the thing that man daily does. It follows, moreover, that all human testimony as well as divine teaching, since couched in human language, is unreliable. The uncertainty of all knowledge, the doubtfulness of all reasoning, the impotency of all conclusions on every subject on which man has ever thought or spoken, are assured, if this principle is once admitted; and so far as truth is concerned truth may be true and we be unable to know it true.

Now it is of course admitted that some witnesses are perjured, and some testimony false, and some reasonings are fallacious, and some conclusions are erroneous. But we men are not lunatics and the human reason is not a fraud. We are so made as to be capable of certainty. We are so constituted as to be able to believe in the integrity of our senses, in the sanity of our minds, and the reliability of our knowledge. We are compelled to believe without a special divine revelation that two and two are four. A thousand miracles from God in attestation would not convince us more fully of it. No added inspiration of all the prophets and apostles would make us more sure of that fact. There is no world in which two and two can make five. In God's mind as in ours two and two are four. We cannot be more certain than we are of this truth—a truth which we know solely by our human faculties.

It is so elsewhere. Trials in the court-room, when conducted under accepted and proved rules of evidence, have reached in many cases a positive conclusion, and the verdict is an absolute certainty; and all who know the evidence are necessarily obliged to own the righteousness of the decision. It would be impossible not to do so. It matters not that there have been sometimes mis-trials and unjust verdicts. The failures only make us more cautious in our legal methods. There is just enough liability to mistake to quicken diligence and make us the more certain of results that are without error. In all processes of investigation, the element of possible mistake is a safeguard against undue haste; an incentive to honest and faithful work. Its outcome, when given due regard, is greater certainty. It serves us, with other human elements, in our investigations by keeping us on our watch against admitting false testimony and coming to rash conclusions. We are so made up by the very constitution of our minds, that we must give credit to evidence, must be convinced by human testimony in certain cases. There is a truthful element in some men's work; a reliability about some kinds of human evidence; a conviction of certainty about results that are attained under some circumstances. This human proof is so absolute that we act upon it in cases where reputation, fortune, and even life itself is involved. About some human things we are certain. They are proved. No more evidence is needed. To have a thing proved, even if the testimony for it is purely human, is the end of all controversy. We are so made as to rely upon sure proof; and we do this, if we have a sound and healthy mind, without one doubt. Now then, if this is so, surely God, in giving us the Bible, will not neglect to give us this very trustworthy form of evidence just where it will be to us the most convincing; just where he has made us to be capable of finding such strong intellectual satisfactions. The Bible knows the men it addresses. Let us be glad that God has made use of this method of proof so reliable elsewhere and so desirable here. To have failed of giving us these mental satisfactions along the line where we certainly should have expected him to meet us, would have appeared very strange and even unreasonable. And though the old adage remains, "to err is human," yet there are circumstances where the theoretical fallibility is practically eliminated from the results—circumstances where a thing proved cannot be more than proved.

We are met, in this human element of the Bible, along the line of our most positive convictions. We are used to this kind of proof, we expect it. We are not foiled in our just anticipations of the certainty to be derived from human testimony. And so, as we gather up the testimony of eye-witnesses, of competent scholars of the olden time, of kings and priests, poets and prophets, evangelists and apostles, we find a peculiarly satisfying proof that God has wrought the work of an inspired volume by human hands. There is a magnificent trend in all this consenting human evidence. The Author of the Bible, who saw the end from the beginning, and who knows what is in man, has consulted our human needs, taken our human methods of proof, and given us evidence along expected and guaranteed lines. He has spoken here in human literature. This human element in the Bible, instead of a source of weakness, is an evidence of strength. It is indeed an argument gained from what some have hastily called an unpromising field. But it is certainly true that the element of supposed fallibility and uncertainty is so managed as to assure us of the carefulness, and so the larger likelihood of accuracy in the biblical writers. And what elsewhere and in some other circumstances would be errancy, becomes under these peculiar conditions a contribution toward a belief in the inerrancy of the book itself.

And yet further; the Bible needs to have the human element in order to be capable of any divine inspiration. There might be a revelation to men who had no written language; but the inspiration of the record of that revelation would need, in order to its existence and accuracy, the human element. It would require literary form of some kind and degree. It would crave some capacity in man to receive and to communicate to others the revelation, however God should make it. This human element is the one on which alone God's

Holy Spirit can lay hold. The Bible must be a human book in order to be an inspired book. We do not subtract from its accuracy, its inerrancy, its infallibility, or its inspiration, when we insist upon this human element. We add the very ingredient that otherwise were wanting. The book is not to be divided into parts, one part human and another part divine. It is not in spots from man, and in other spots from God. To be of God anywhere it must everywhere be of man. Mr. Spurgeon has said: "The eternal Word, Jesus Christ, is both human and divine, but no man can say where the divine ends and the human begins. So in the written word of God, every word is both human and divine in source; but no man can define the limits between the human and the divine."

A revelation without human means is indeed conceivable. There is revelation in suns and stars, in mountains and plains. There was revelation at Horeb and Carmel. But inspiration requires man in the use of his mental powers. It is mind moving upon mind; soul in contact with soul; one personality projecting itself upon another; one person's thought and feeling, and it may be his words, entering into another's thinking and feeling and speech. It is one person affecting another; but not so that the personality of the other is always and necessarily suspended. In some cases, it may be, it renders the human mind more acute, more susceptible, and more self-conscious. A man would not be less a man but more completely a man by the inspiration of God. In some few forms of the inspiring influence, as in the case of prophecy, the requirement may have been for exaltation beyond one's self.

And yet it has been earnestly contended that all distant prophecies see a nearer point of human vision and a nearer material fulfillment as their first meaning; while the far-off vision is that of things seen as having no chronological, but only a logical relation; events seen as connected in order of kind rather than in order of time. Let us leave it for heathen nations to believe in a "divine afflatus," seizing upon men in moments of delirium, when the mind is off its balance. The lunatic and the man bereft momentarily of his reason they thought more likely to be inspired. The frenzy of idol worshipers was at the farthest remove from the moral sanity of the prophets of Jehovah. The *séances* of the so-called "spiritualist" of our day, wherein the pretence is of the overpowering of the medium's mind by some "spirit," are the exact opposite of the sacred occasions on which holy men spoke as moved by God. The paroxysms of nervous devotees may be ascribed to heathen gods and to imaginary "spirits." But a grand sanity is the preparation of Moses and Isaiah and Matthew and John for divine inspiration. To be "in the Spirit" is not to be out of one's mind. Sense rather than nonsense is a characteristic of biblical inspiration. Men wise with holy moral wisdom, whose minds grow large and clear in the radiance of God, whose hearts grow warm under holy love and whose hands and feet are swift at his service, are the ones most likely to be used by the Holy Spirit of God. These men of the former ages, far from being perfect in personal character, were yet the best men in their centuries. They were the foremost moral souls, and so were likely to get the best of the coming advance. They stood highest and so were more certain to be struck by the earlier rays of the Sun of Righteousness. Not folly but wisdom, not vice but virtue, not fanaticism but sense, not ecstatic convulsion but the steady moral sanity of men calmly but earnestly engaged in God's work—these were for the most part the human characteristics to be seized upon, enlarged, purified, guided, and inspired by the Holy Ghost.

Here too, as everywhere else, we can but mark the inspiring activity seeking its end. There is steady advance in moral vision. The writers are in a series, and one growing movement sweeps them on. The breath of God breathes on these broad historic fields where we find them. They bend, like the yellow corn in autumnal days, when stirred by the breeze. You can see the direction of the wind and watch its progress over the billowy plains. These men are always looking on. The vital eye is always growing sharper. You can see each steadily growing in a better inspiration than the one he supersedes. Moses, one of the older, is always the grandest soul personally among all the men from Adam to Jesus. But the inspiration of inferior men, farther on in the series, is more advanced than his. Isaiah sees farther and gives his age a proto-gospel. David, inferior in moral fibre, reaches higher planes than those trod by the grander man who led Israel from

Egypt in that most memorable march. For, while the inspiring spirit selects best souls, the age must also be consulted; and the inspiration advances, though no second Moses appears, till Christ comes. So that the inspiration of God is the agency more potent than grandeur of powers or personal piety. The later prophets see more than their greater sire at Pharaoh's court. The divine trend is stronger than the human personality. The increasing light of divine inspiration is not negligent of goodness, and yet is not measured in its degree by the piety of the man inspired.

And when the inspiring spirit ceases this peculiar work because the book is completed, the whole matter of its preservation as so much human literature is left to the operation of the same laws as govern other productions. The eliminating process went on. The more ancient documents seem to have perished, except as these books of the Bible, differing from all others in their moral purpose, took up and preserved the best portions of them. It was an instance of the survival of the fittest. It was the law of tendency. It was natural selection with a moral purpose in it. It kept itself afloat on the stream of time while other literature sank into oblivion. It is true that there was human genius—if you will, a human inspiration in it; so that the best Hebrew minds, those most likely to be touched by the earlier rays of a divine inspiration, were the immortal ones whose memorable works still reflect the light.

And just because it is human work on one side of it, this book is exposed to the same fate as other noble literature. As in Homer and Virgil, and even in our later Shakespeare, there are various readings, so the manuscripts occasionally differ, though taken as a whole they have wonderful agreement. It was fitting that a book just as distinctly man's book in some of its features as any other, should be treated in the same way as all other ancient writings, so far as its preservation is concerned. We need not deny a divine providence in the preservation of a book which has in it also a divine element. But we should expect that the human in the Scriptures, produced according to the laws of literary method, should be left in the main to do battle with destructive agencies, exactly as are other volumes of a similar antiquity.

The fact of a human element, left in part to our human preservation, is the warrant for a scholarly work which is sometimes known as the " higher criticism." No name could have been more unfortunate, awaking as it does instant prejudice and opposition. The men who have given themselves to questions that relate to a genuine test for the Hebrew and Greek Scriptures, are not more lofty in aim nor of higher scholarship than other biblical scholars. One section of these workers have confessedly given up prayer. But prayerlessness in such inquiries is not only unsympathetic but unscholarly. If the undevout astronomer is mad, what shall be said of the undevout biblical critic? But we must remember that the destructive critic is not the only nor even the superior critic. The questions about documents and dates and origins and authors, about books as composite and as reedited, are not new. The great scholars of former times debated them. But they would not have allowed themselves to be called by any such name as "higher critics," nor permitted their work to be called the "higher criticism." Of large learning, the equals of any men now living, they sifted and compared and judged. They decided on the authenticity and inspiration of the books admitted to the canon. Their method was absolutely logical before the more modern names of the "inductive" and "deductive" methods were bestowed upon certain processes of human thought. It was not in late centuries that men began to reason. There were scholars before our own day. Learning did not begin with the latter half of the nineteenth century.

But though assumption in these respects has awakened prejudice, we must not yield ourselves to any reactionary mood. God committed these documents to his churches; and the questions about dates and places and texts and versions are all of importance. Hitherto the discussion of them has tended on the whole to confirm rather than unsettle. And it will do so we believe in time to come. Plain Christians may at first be somewhat disturbed. But the final result has always been helpful. The foundations stand secure. Whatever of light from linguistic criticism or archæological discovery we can gain for the better understanding of the Bible, we most gladly welcome. And we owe to devout students along these lines a great debt of gratitude; for while not denying the divine element, they have called back attention to the human element which early Christian scholars had made prominent, but which without doubt has not for the past few centuries received sufficient emphasis.[1] And if occasionally a devout man, in this reaction against undue emphasis in the one direction, has gone too far in the other, the aim and spirit of the genuine student may be named in extenuation. Great scholars in

---

[1] In the "Homiletic Review" for January, 1895, Prof. Henry Preserved Smith claims certain results for the "Higher Criticism." They are 1: "The composite nature of the Historical Books." But the fact of composite material was taught by leading professors in our theological seminaries half a century ago. 2. "The composite authorship of the Psalms." But the version we have all used for years has as a prefatory remark to the ninetieth psalm, "A Psalm of Moses, the man of God"; while such headings as these are found, "A Psalm of Asaph," "A Psalm of the sons of Korah," "A Psalm of Solomon." Surely the ancient division of the psalms into five books is no new discovery. And their characterization as "Psalms of David," as "Davidic," as "of the times of Josiah," "of the age of Ezra and Nehemiah," is far from being modern. The assignment may not be accurate, but it is certainly ancient. And he would be very bold in assertion who would say that the last word had been spoken on the date or on the authorship of the Psalms. 3. "The wisdom literature." But here too, modern investigators are simply treading in old footsteps. It will be news, indeed, that scholarship for centuries has not recognized the fact that Solomon was not the sole author of the "Proverbs" and of the "wisdom literature" in general. 4. "The post-exilic date of the final redaction of the Pentateuch." But even here it is to be noted that so old a commentator as good, pious Matthew Henry, in his note on Deut. 34, says, "This chapter was written by Joshua or Eleazar or, as Patrick conjectures, by Samuel, who was a prophet, and wrote by divine authority." So that these questions are neither newly raised nor newly "decided." They are, and are likely to be, in the flux of discussion, and neither the ancient nor the modern dogmatism on them is warranted. Meanwhile, careful men wait. But whatever the outcome, whether of certainty or uncertainty, nothing essential is really disturbed. The human element is purposely left as it is by divine wisdom.

former times have erred here and there in details; but their general work has been of immense worth to the Christian world. And modern scholars may have announced prematurely their conclusions in biblical science, exactly as scholarly men have done in medical and in natural science. We do not therefore distrust and discard investigation. The general trend in these investigations is unmistakable. The things surrendered are few, the facts gained are many. The book is a divine development through good men moved upon by the Holy Spirit.

In the preceding section it is argued that in order that the Bible might be capable of being an inspired volume, it must have in it the human element. It was certainly written by men in possession of their human faculties. Its historic portions bear evidence of having been composed under the same mental conditions as are exhibited in uninspired books. Its writers gathered evidence. They took the testimony often of eye-witnesses. They were capable of being inspired by the Spirit of God, since they were possessed of mental and moral faculties. Is the other proposition also true, viz.: that the divine element is required to make the human element reliable in such a book as the Bible?

Section II. The Divine Element

Suppose we consider that what is chiefly and primarily inspired is a great series of connected facts, partly common and partly uncommon. These facts constitute Hebrew history and culminate in

THE HUMAN AND THE DIVINE ELEMENTS

Jesus Christ and his apostles. It might at first be thought that the ordinary facts in this series would require only the human element in the record of them, while divine inspiration might be needed for those which were supernatural. But what if the ordinary facts are so related to the extraordinary, the common to the supernatural, and both so related to the great underlying plan of them, and so connected with the divinely unifying thought that throbs through them all, that the kind of narrative which is required needs the divine supervision in the smallest as well as in largest things. In a narrative of things so related to each other and to one great plan, the divine element is needed to correct the human.

Out of my window in the city I look and see two men engaged in an altercation on the street below. From my position I see it all and see it accurately. Toward the combatants runs a reporter from a side street and sees one part of the affair. Soon comes another and he sees the middle of the transaction. Both come to my room to make up their notes, knowing that I have seen the whole affair and am able to judge accurately of the quarrel. Each writing honestly of what he has seen is liable to use some word or phrase which does not correctly represent the matter. I do not write one word of their report, but I supervise the whole. If a single preposition gives a wrong impression, I suggest a better and they adopt it.

Let us open the Bible and take an incident at random that is not miraculous. It shall be the fact of Jesus going to dine on the Sabbath at a

Pharisee's house. That incident can be recorded in such a way as to be entirely out of sympathy with the whole plan of Christ's life. Without using one false word a writer can so set down the incident as to smirch the whole character of Jesus Christ. It can be so recorded that the Lord will seem to be a Sabbath breaker. It can make him a glutton. It can make him a winebibber. It can make him favor Pharisaism. It can leave the impression that he courted the rich at the expense of the poor. It can invert every principle on which his character was founded. Two or three such scenes described in unfortunate language would not only neutralize the power of any incident for good, but make it a positive harm in all the coming centuries. Superintendence to bring the record into line with God's dominating thought is clearly needed. The fact to all the world, save the few nearest concerned, is the fact as seen in the record of the Gospels. A single unguarded word in the record would leave the wrong impression on the ages. Even in common things the tone of the narrative means more than the facts themselves.

Hallam's personal thought in his "Constitutional History" tinges every fact he names. Green in his "History of the English People" cannot conceal if he would his whole point of view. His tone is as distinct as are his facts. In the Bible the inspired facts are in line of an inspired Divine thought. The Thinker must guide the free writer in every turn of a sentence, or as well have no inspired fact and thought. Did you ever stand beside the pilot of a noble ship as she plowed the billows, a thing of life? Did you ever watch his eye as it glanced at the compass, then up at the sails, then over the side as he saw the coming wave? If everything goes right he stands motionless. But if he sees that a flaw of the freshening wind is about to change his vessel's prow but a trifle from the true course, how quickly he causes the turn of the wheel to meet the new deflecting force. Or if a broad wave gathering on her quarter is about to strike his ship from the line of her progress, swiftly the wheel is reversed. And thus amid all the disturbing influences of wind and wave the pilot guides the ship surely and safely in her unchanged path. So God guides the men through whom he will make known his will. Amid all human imperfections, amid the veering of winds and the tossing of the waves the helmsman never steers wildly, never loses his control, never is deflected from his course. Man's book has God's superintendence in all its parts.

And when we come to the miraculous, this, though not more necessary, is even more evident. Human writers unassisted in their record of the supernatural are sure to blunder. They are competent witnesses of fact. They would be good annalists. But the historian is far more than a writer of annals. The Gospels are histories. They are connected narratives infused with a thought. No honesty could save an unassisted writer from mistake by some turn of a phrase, some ill-judged and inaccurate word in describing the miraculous. For the miracle does not stand alone. It has fit time, place, and circumstance. It has its distinctive character, its peculiar setting in the teaching, its unique position in the divine evolution of the divine idea. A miracle is never a mere buttress. It is not even a stone in the foundation. It is a thing growing out of the system. It is not a support of the revelation, but a development in it. It is moral fact incarnate in physical form. It will have to be handled with care in the record. If the primary inspiration is in the fact as one of a series, the inspiration in the thought comes close upon it; and both demand superintendence, guidance, correction, accuracy.

And surely no one can dispute the ability of God so to inspire men. That he can leave them free to write and yet can guide their writing is, to say the least, possible. We may go further and claim its probability. We are warranted by the former citations in these discussions to claim this as a fact. Nor is the fact invalidated because the same thing does not occur in the experience of any or of all men to-day. It is not to be understood as the normal condition of mankind, nor of these writers of the Scriptures. Not at all times were they commanded, "Write the things thou sawest in a book." Not always when Jeremiah speaks does the Lord say, "Stand in the gate and proclaim this word" (Jer. 7 : 1). Not of all Moses may write, is it said that "the book of the law" is to be "put into the ark." Isaiah doubtless wrote many a sentence; but it is only of a certain series of things that he is told to "Write it in a book." Not always is the prophetic hand of Elisha on the arm of Joash as he draws the bow. But the inspiring Spirit at times made use of the chosen instrument. That he should select foremost men to reveal truth by them is only what we should expect. In other departments than religion the action of great genius in its highest reaches is often a wonder to the men themselves and can scarcely be understood by others. It is easier to describe than to define what is meant by human inspiration as known to poet, musician, orator, and writer. They know, but they cannot tell it. Even as to those sudden intuitions, discoveries, disclosures, those revelations of the mind to itself as to the way in which a given thing can best be done; that surprising insight which in some gifted moments enables men to see what was dark before, that quick flash of sunlight on the perplexity that had baffled our study for days and weeks; that unraveling and clearing of a tangled skein of thought; that glad heart-throb when an idea is born, a thought struck out, an invention perfected —even as to these inspirations of human genius, it is not easy to offer any careful and exact definition. The great inventors and discoverers and poets and painters and orators cannot tell you what it is they feel. They can only give us some general account of the state of mind in which they are when seized upon with the idea which they have given to the world. They say it must be felt in order to be understood.[1]

---

[1] Mozart describing the state of mind in which musical composition was to him most lively and successful says: "Then, the thoughts come streaming in upon me most fluently, whence or

Now if we take the case of the most extreme demand for a divine inspiration, viz., that of prophecy, we can gain, from these intimations given in human inspiration, some reassuring hints. We can see its trend. In most cases, some would claim in all, the prophets were in their sanest moods. Conscious of more than self, they do not lose self-consciousness. It shows that the divine inspiration did not so enwrap them as to destroy or even distort the usual operations of their minds, when we find them while under its influence affected normally as well. The case of Ezekiel, who remained "astonished for seven days" (Ezek. 3 : 15) shows the man in full possession of his usual faculties. He is not receiving any mechanical inspiration. He is no "rapt seer." He understands enough of his own message to be profoundly stirred thereby. He is no passive "amanuensis," no mere "pen of God," no mere "scribe of an unknown influence," no "machine for God's touch." He has intelligent consciousness of what is going on about him and revealed in him. He has not been "lost in an overpowering inspiration."

Daniel, by his river Ulai, was also "astonished" at his vision (Dan. 8 : 27). Habakkuk "trembled" as he foretold the terrors God would bring according to his words; and when mercy was shown him as sure to come to his people at their repentance, he cried out, "I will greatly rejoice in the

---

how is more than I can tell. Then follows the clang of the different instruments; then, if not disturbed, the thing grows greater, broader, clearer. I see the whole like a beautiful picture. This is delight."

Lord." We need not deny a verbal, if we reject a mechanical theory of the divinely prophetic influence. We may decline to accept any theory, holding ourselves closely to the facts. Enough in this connection to note that the prophets never claim to be other than themselves. They are men; but men inspired of God.

On the other hand, while not losing their consciousness, they do not always understand all their words contain. The meaning of their message must not be fully measured by what they understood of it. It had a fullness beyond them and often beyond their day. They saw the nearer, but not always the farther fact. It is merely a curious question for us to inquire how far they and the men of their time understood prophecies which were to be full of unfolding for all time and eternity. The larger and better question for us is not what they thought, but what is God's thought in these prophecies. Message is larger than messenger. All time is larger than their time. God's intention rather than their understanding is our inquiry as we study the words that came from him. To read such words, shutting off God above and the Christian centuries beyond, and to ask only how they and the men of their time would understand them, may be good secular scholarship, but it is not biblical scholarship. It will do in other history with merely secular documents as its basis, but not here. Here, to leave out the inspiration of God, is to seek sunlight by ignoring the sun.

Caiaphas uttered a prophecy. He meant one thing by it, God meant another. He intended to incite to murder. God's spirit in the record explains the profound intimation of Christ's sacrificial death given through the official head of the Hebrew hierarchy. "This he spake not of himself, but being high priest that year, he prophesied that Jesus should die for that nation, and not for that nation only, but that also he should gather together in one the children of God that were scattered abroad." In this case at least the inspiration must have extended to the words themselves. It shows God's choice of an author, Caiaphas. It shows a thought in God's mind wholly different from that in the mind of the human author. This instance, though peculiar in some aspects, is singularly instructive as a whole. It is a passage urged with great force by those who would put a special emphasis on inspiration as found mainly in the words. They urge that in this instance and in a few others in which bad men are divinely inspired we are shown that inspiration is sometimes in the language rather than in the man, and that the divine authority is co-extensive with the writing. They urge that the only instance in which the specific word "inspiration" occurs, names not the thought but the writing; that it is the "scripture," *i. e.* the writing, and not the sense of it, that is "God-inspired." It may be true that the words are usually accompanied by the thought on the part of the writer, but not always so, and not in any case necessarily so.[1] And yet may not these few

---

[1] Those who hold to "verbal" inspiration, *i. e.*, inspiration of words, are wont to quote the opening words of Leviticus, "And Jehovah called unto Moses," the word denotes "speaking with

instances be unduly pressed? May they not be "the exception that proves the rule"? They simply do not show the usual process of divine inspiration through a sympathetic soul. And if the general language of the Bible in such phrases as "thus saith the Lord" would at first reading seem to lay an emphasis upon words, it by no means excludes the underlying thought. Possibly we cannot have a theory broad enough to cover every instance. We are not bound to have any theory that is hard and fast on this subject. We see facts. We trace a trend. The trend is from God. Dr. Garbett (Boyle Lectures, 1862) says: "The kind of this divine guidance may vary in the different portions of the written word. But it can never be lacking to any part. The divine inspiration will not be found in portions here and there, but like the human element it will be everywhere in such a book recording such a series of facts as is the Bible. The one all-pervading element is as needful as the other; nor in such a

---

an audible voice." If this be allowed, then the method in this particular book is that of direct oral dictation. It is claimed that this is primarily an inspiration of words, and only secondarily of thought. But the further question of the inspiration of the writing out of these inspired words which had been dictated is still open. And such usage in one case would not settle the question in other cases. And yet the whole book of Leviticus is dictated, except in two brief episodes, viz., the consecration of Aaron and the punishment of two priests. Perhaps this case, so unlike that usual elsewhere in which reason, memory, judgment, and personality are all employed, will best illustrate the view urged in a former chapter, that no one theory of inspiration can be carried consistently through the entire Bible. Trend covers all theories with its recognition of each of them as having an element of truth.

book can you have the one without the other. The divine element, or the part belonging to God in the composition of the sacred Scripture, is to be maintained with equal distinctness.

"This divine element includes (1) the selection of the writers, with their special peculiarities of circumstance and character for their given work, and their education for it; (2) their instruction in the subject-matter of their writings, alike by the revelation of what was previously unknown to them, by the verification of knowledge possessed by them through ordinary human channels, and by the selection of the things to be written and the things to be omitted from the writing. As a general rule the sacred writers were conscious and intelligent agents, understanding more or less perfectly the meaning of their own message; but cases have been specifically excepted in order to prevent our limiting the sense of the words written by the intention of the human writers. These two instances are found in John 11 : 15 and 1 Peter 1 : 11.

"Hence it follows that the divine element includes (3) the guidance of the Spirit in the selection of the words employed by the sacred writers. If the divine inspiration acted only in communicating truth to the sacred writers, and did not extend to their communication of this divinely given truth to others, it is certain that we possess only a human account of a divine revelation, and not the very revelation itself. The veracity of the truth transmitted must be equivalent, neither more nor less, to the accuracy of the words which convey it; (4)

it involves the absolute truth of all the things written. Man is fallible, and liable to make mistakes; but actually to make mistakes is as unnecessary to the completeness of the human element as not to make mistakes is absolutely essential to the divine. The Bible may be truly the work of man, and yet be true; but if it be not certainly true it cannot also be the work of God. The concurrence of the human part of Scripture and the divine part of Scripture is thus perfect throughout. It is not, however, the concurrence of two equals, but of a superior and an inferior. Man is necessarily the subordinate instrument and God necessarily the originating and controlling agent. Hence it follows that as the existence of what is divine in Scripture is no sound argument against its being human, so the existence of what is human in Scripture is no sound argument against its also being divine."

In a former section the claims made by the Scriptures themselves to a divine inspiration have been set forth. So too the claims of the New Testament that "all Scripture," *i. e.*, Old Testament, "is given by inspiration of God," have been cited. Christ's promise to inspire has been examined; and the declarations of apostolic writers that their words were not merely human but the word of God, have been perhaps sufficiently quoted. The only exception alleged is that in which Paul for a specific thing alleges that he speaks rather than the Lord, *i. e.*, the Lord Jesus Christ. But he is applying principles in which one may not follow unbending rules aside from circumstances. So far from denying his own inspiration, he asserts that the Lord allows him to give advice rather than command; that some things the Lord, *i. e.*, the Lord Jesus, did not during his earthly life, expressly enjoin. Indeed the whole drift of the apostle in the few cases cited is to assert in the most positive form his inspiration elsewhere as direct; and in these cases to assert his inspiration as inspired advice in matters where Jesus had not laid down express commandment. The Holy Spirit may equally inspire both command and counsel.

But in addition to the direct promises of Jesus,[1] the position in which the apostles found themselves as representatives of the new religion after their Lord's departure is one of such singular responsibility that they could not do without large measures of the inspiring Spirit. They needed this inspiration not only in writing but in planning and in directing. This was their constant reliance in their work. They were to take no special thought or care, but it was to be given them what to say; and the ground of this singular prohibition and promise was, " it shall be the Spirit of your Father that speaketh in you." They were to be endued for their work "with the power from on high."

---

[1] The promised inspiration to apostles is recorded in John 14 : 16, 17, 26; 15 : 26, 27; 16 : 13–15; Acts 1 : 8; Matt. 16 : 18, 19; 18 : 18; John 20 : 22, 23; Matt. 10 : 19, 20; Mark 13 : 11; Luke 12 : 11, 12.

The corresponding claims of the apostles may be found in such scriptures as Acts 4 : 8; 11 : 12; 15 : 28; 1 Peter 1 : 12; Gal. 1 : 11–24; 2 : 1–14; 1 Cor. 1 : 1; 1 Cor. 2 : 7, 10–13; 14 : 36, 37; 2 Cor. 3 : 4–6; Gal. 2 : 6–9; 2 Peter 3 : 15, 16; Rev. 1 : 10, 11.

THE HUMAN AND THE DIVINE ELEMENTS

The time when they should "be able to bear it" had now come, and Jesus was fulfilling his own promise to them of inspiration, as he led them "into all truth." Oral speaking as well as written word was equally included. Of the two, the latter was evidently the more important. A mistake in the one might be corrected, but documents could not be amended. The writers ask credence on the ground of special inspiration, but not on the ground of special probity or of peculiar piety. The idea of any special "genius for religion" seems never to have occurred to them. They talk constantly of being "led by the Spirit" in the places whither they go, and of special momentary direction of what they shall speak. The tone is unmistakable. They claim that those who are of God will hear them. And accordingly the early Christians did actually receive them on that claim.

It was not that they were mentally and morally above others, nor their writings of higher literary or moral worth in themselves. Their writings were accepted and honored as the depositories of God's Spirit. These books were called "Holy Scriptures," "Divine Scriptures," "Scriptures of the Lord," "Divine Oracles," "Oracles of the Lord," "Old and New Oracles," "Sacred Fountains," etc., while other books of Christian writers were never so called. All the early sects accepted certain books as of scriptural authority. All appealed to them as final, on the ground of their inspiration. The phrase, "Thus saith the Holy Spirit" is one used by the apostolic Fathers in quoting these books, and the primitive Fathers represent denial of the inspiration of these books, whether of the Old or the New Testament, as infidelity. This acceptance at so early a date of these writings as inspired is significant. For we can understand how possibly later ages might have done this, when centuries of veneration had gathered about them. But that the very generation which heard the story, and those immediately succeeding, should have so done, is to be attributed to two things: the universal knowledge that this inspiration had been promised by Christ, and that it was directly claimed by these writers. And were we further to remember that it was no easy thing for Jews, even for converted Jews, to put the New Testament writers on the same level with the honored prophets of their lifelong veneration, the only explanation of their belief was that they knew the broad promise and were ready for the broad fulfillment.

CHAPTER VI

DIFFICULTIES AND CONFIRMATIONS

THERE are difficulties in the Bible. These difficulties are urged as objections to its inspiration. The book covers long centuries in which there were various ways of computing historic times and of recording historic events. It uses dissimilar literary methods, which an inexact student is likely to confuse. It employs necessarily the peculiar forms of expression which were known in the time of a given writer. And these peculiar expressions of one age grew to be somewhat obscure in the next ages, and in a few centuries they formed a difficulty for common readers. But slowly the students of the Bible and of contemporaneous documents are getting to see that these very difficulties are really confirmations. The objections change sides and become delightful auxiliaries of faith. Some still remain unsolved. But the past experience with difficulties more vexing than any that now remain, warrants us in hoping, in all cases now existing, for a happy solution. As we get back in our thought and feeling to the former times, as we put ourselves in the places of the men then living, we get abundant confirmation of the authenticity of the book, a better guaranteed belief that it was written in the times and circumstances which it claims for itself, and a larger faith in that marvelous trend by which it is separated, worldwide, from all other literature.

Some of these difficulties, which carefully considered become confirmations, must now be noticed.

This element in the Old Testament has occasioned not a little adverse criticism. God speaks like a man. He does not at all times accord well with our later standards. He walks. He talks. He is represented as if having a body. He repents. He grows angry. He varies in mood. He takes pleasure in the fragrance of odors. He has meats set before him. He is propitiated by blood. He smiles. He frowns. He makes choices seemingly capricious. He directs wars. He orders slaughter; he is very human. It is the Homeric and the ante-Homeric method of representing the participation of the gods in the affairs of men. The tone is peculiar. Jehovah may have, like the olden gods, a heaven, and yet he is here among men suddenly and swiftly in all their extremities.

Section I. Anthropomorphism

But let any student of the old Latin or Greek classics tell us what he would think of these poems if anthropomorphic ways of speaking had been omitted. The absence of this style would be positive proof that the said poems were not of the date ascribed to them. These ways of representation are the literary method of the age. They are exactly the forms of speech then used. They become confirmations of the alleged age in which the poems were produced. The insertion of modern ways of speech would be fatal to their genuineness. In like manner the Bible in its older parts must use the conceptions of the older times. In no other way could those ages receive any teaching at all. It was necessary to begin on their literary level and work upward.

But, though these forms of speech abound in the Bible, the conception is never that of a plurality of gods. One God, the creator of the heaven and the earth, the Sovereign Ruler of things and men, is the uniform presentation. He is from the outset a moral God. He is the foe of wrong, the friend of right. Expressions are often anthropomorphic, and as such have their deficiency. But it is not moral deficiency. The biblical ideas throb through the language which itself would restrict them. Never is the defectiveness wrongfulness.

Then too, consider how surely the childhood of each age seizes on these expressions which some would condemn. They are graphic words to the boy. He must have them. You cannot teach him without using them. They get hold of his head and heart. They are the best for him, all things considered. He will find objections to them by and by, as he will about a hundred other forms of speech. If he ever becomes a student of idiomatic language, the old familiar figures of speech will all be analyzed by him; and every one of them be equally faulty. But he must begin with what he finds. And he must take the methods which all other children take in all other ages, when they begin to think and talk of God.

Nor will the boy grown to manhood ever quite decline to use this language. He may fill it full of spiritual meaning, but he will retain the old anthropomorphic forms. In prayer the grown man will be obliged to use them. He will ask God to "look down propitiously," "to bend his ear," "to lift up the light of his countenance," "to reach out his hand," "to bestow his blessing," "to guard," "to watch,"—all of which are anthropomorphic words. So too it is with all those mental and moral phrases derived from our own human faculties and ascribed to God. We are his image in mind and soul; and though in the progress of ideas we get a broader conception and fuller expression, we do not so much leave the older forms of language behind as give them new richness through better spiritualization. In the New Testament we find their use continued. And while their graphic force is not lessened, they are infused with a more gracious meaning. The newer, fuller conception animates the old words. The tendency is always to larger and better conceptions of God. The imperfect was not the erroneous in the olden time. It serves to-day as the large outline to be filled out by the same spirit in the new dispensation.

Section II. Chronology

Difficulties about historical time do certainly exist in all old literature—the Bible not excepted. In a book made up as is the Bible, not on the lines of a connected history but by appropriating all forms of literary work, these difficulties are largely increased. The date of events and the time of their records are very distinct matters of inquiry; and yet often the differences, while not of the least moral importance, are fair questions for literary criticism. Sometimes, however, large moral questions are involved in this matter of dates. Not infrequently there are widely different ways of reckoning time in the documents which supplied the material for the writers. Persian and Babylonian, Assyrian and Egyptian dates are given, each starting from a different point, each computed in a different way. Occasionally "round numbers" are used in a speech, and the orator's words are taken down and so are liable to be considered as chronologically, rather than oratorically, accurate. The Hebrew nation had not itself always the same way of noting the day and the hour, while much that occurred before that national life began has only some general claim to historic order. The writers had the Semitic carefulness about facts and carelessness about dates. Even in the New Testament the Gospel writers sometimes mass their material so as to set forth a peculiar aspect of Christ, so as to present him now as the miracle worker and now as the moral teacher. The Gospels are historic in form, but they are *memorabilia* in fact. The writers gather incidents in a fair, general order; not, indeed, confusing years, but still leaving open the question, in one case at least, as to what "feast" is meant in a given verse. Questions of harmony seem never to have been considered; and orderly arrangement, in some cases, is evidently subordinate to the special object of the writer.

But in the older parts of the Old Testament this negligence of dates in important matters seems very strange until we put ourselves back in the place of the writers. The method of record seems to be that of the simple graphic statement of a fact. The time of the occurrence is often assumed as known to the men who first saw the narration. And even when the Pentateuch is left there are historic difficulties. The only wonder is that we do not find more. Take a single instance which shows the liability to mistake in the writing of numbers. In 1 Samuel 6 : 19 we read of "fifty thousand threescore and ten men," where it is impossible that there should have been any such number. But the Hebrew and Arabic languages permit us to write first the units and then the tens and then the hundreds, or to reverse the order, and to write the highest first. Hence it is equally competent to write "seventy" and "fifty" and "a thousand"—which may mean either as given in our version, or it may mean simply one thousand one hundred and seventy. In such latitude of usage there is immense liability to sad over-statements in translation.[1]

A considerable number of alleged inaccuracies

---

[1] In a note on 1 Samuel 6, by Dr. Kirkpatrick, in "Cambridge Bible," we read: "Such errors as this, to which the text of any ancient book is liable in process of transmission, do not affect the general trustworthiness of the narrative; and the freest acknowledgment of them in no way precludes the full belief in the inspiration of the Scriptures."

In view of instances like this, Dr. J. R. Thompson says: "Chronology is peculiarly difficult when we have to do with Oriental modes of computation, which are essentially different from ours."

have been pointed out by men hospitable to objections. But most reverent and thoughtful students, taking into view all the facts, will find their number greatly reduced. Of these one, one only, is still to many a stumbling-block. Acts 7: 14-16 is held by some to be a statement clearly erroneous on its face. But even if this solitary instance were utterly inexplicable, it would by no means follow that some missing factor may not yet be found, as in the case of other difficulties which vexed us half a century ago. To call in question the accuracy and inspiration of all the other books of the Bible because of a mistake which is possibly ours and not that of the Scripture, were certainly unjust. And even in this case, there may be found a solution, if we shall grant that the words are so evident and palpable a verbal inaccuracy as to stand out as such alike to the speaker and to those who heard him. For the speaker is thoroughly familiar with the real facts as they lie on the face of the story in the Old Testament, and the hearers of Stephen knew them as well as he. He speaks freely, generally, without the idea that a single hearer will contradict him. He clearly speaks what they believe. And even if he had spoken erroneously, Luke, who records the speech, knew the facts of the biblical history. In some way or other the Old and the New stories must be harmonious to such persons. The greatness of the mistake shows that it can have no argumentative weight. In some familiarity of speech, generally accepted by the people of Stephen's time, he spoke; and in the same familiarity they heard.

The chief inaccuracies alleged are (1) seventy-five persons are named, when only seventy are given in Genesis 46: 27. There is a suggested explanation in the fact that Joseph may have "called for" seventy-five to go to Egypt, not knowing of the death of Jacob's wives and that of Judah's sons. So too, if the Septuagint was quoted by Stephen, it may have added the sons of Ephraim and Manasseh. The number "called for" in one narrative and the number that actually "went down into Egypt" are respectively seventy-five and seventy. Each writer tells of the same transaction viewed from the standpoint of differing years. So seen, the discrepancy becomes a confirmation. The more of such "mistakes" the better when we see the seventeen years and the changed facts which intervene. Says another: "The idea of mistake is excluded by the fact that both numbers, seventy and seventy-five, were known to the Jews. Philo mentions them and moralizes according to his fashion on both the numbers. The Septuagint (the Greek translation of the Old Testament made between 300 and 250 B. C.) gives the number seventy-five in Genesis 46: 27, where the Hebrew speaks of seventy. This number the Greek translators have made up by adding, in verse 20, to the sons of Joseph, grandchildren and great grandchildren to the number of five, thus making the whole seventy-five instead of seventy. Now, why should they change the number in the Hebrew original? And why, having changed it, should they mass the descendants of Joseph together in this way? If they must alter, why not take Judah or Levi, the two tribes we might have expected to be specially favored? The answer to this question solves our difficulty. There was evidently another and more usual reckoning among the people than the number given in Genesis, and the Greek translators altered the reading to suit it. Seventy was the number when Jacob went down to Egypt. But seventeen years afterward, when he was dying, the great father of the race altered the arrangement of the tribes. (See Gen. 48 : 5, 6.)

"The consequence of this new disposition of the tribes was that Manasseh and Ephraim were placed among the great fathers of the race; and that, just as the immediate descendants of the other patriarchs who were living at the time of the going down into Egypt were numbered, so the descendants of Ephraim and Manasseh, alive at the time when Jacob gave them this inheritance, were also numbered and added to the previous seventy. These were five, and we are indebted to the Septuagint for having preserved their names. Seventy-five in this way displaced in the traditions of Israel the seventy of the reckoning in Gen. 46 : 27.

"The recollection of the honor done to Joseph was kept alive by God throughout the ages. The references to it in Scripture are frequent. In Psalm 77 : 15, we read, 'Thou hast with thine arm redeemed thy people, the sons of Jacob and Joseph.' It will be noted how the sons of Joseph are set here alongside the sons of Jacob as forming the great assembly of the people of God.

They are two bands, the one taking its place by descent, the other by grace. In 1 Chron. 5 : 1, 2, we learn that Jacob's gift was the bestowal of a lapsed birthright. Reuben had lost it by his sin : 'his birthright was given unto the sons of Joseph, the son of Israel.'

"Now Stephen's argument necessarily led him to take the number which told especially of Joseph's triumph. The story of Joseph is a parallel to that of Jesus. He was rejected by his brethren, and yet, among those very brethren, this great place was at last accorded to him. This difficulty, therefore, like many another, was an indication of the existence of a neglected truth; and the supposed mistake is simply a proof of the clear and vivid thought by which that great speech of his is throughout inspired." [1]

Another inaccuracy from the same speech is the alleged "burial of Jacob at Sychem, whereas in Gen. 49, it is said that he was buried at Hebron." But the words are in the plural, "were carried over and laid" and the Revised version reads : " They"—the bones of the fathers—"were carried over and laid." Nor is there anything in either Testament to the contrary. The carrying of the bones to Sychem is affirmed by Jewish tradition and was a matter of belief in the days of Stephen.

Another alleged inaccuracy in the story is the substitution of the word Abraham for Jacob in the speech as given by Luke. But it must be re-

---

[1] Rev. J. Urquart, in "Preacher's Magazine," May, 1894.

membered that the Jews of that age—witness also the respective and disagreeing genealogies in Matthew and Luke—were fond of giving their own well-known history in rapid sketches, in brief formulas, in which, as in the tables of genealogy, events were quoted in series of equal numbers. An ancestor, sometimes remote, gives name to what was done by descendants. This method of speaking, which causes us a difficulty, was nothing of the sort to that age, when the Jews were rehearsing the well-known national history. Dr. Hackett names the theory of Davidson that there was a verbal error in Stephen's speech, which the accurate Luke perpetuates, though knowing it to be such, so intent is he in recording exactly what Stephen did say on that occasion. "It is, however," says Hackett, "difficult to resist the impression that a single word of the present text is wrong." In such a case, those described by Dr. E. G. Robinson as "over-anxious to recognize what they call ignorance or prejudice on the part of the writers of the Scriptures," have their choice instance. But thousands of careful and scholarly men would rather see here, as in the text of other ancient authors, an error by some copyist in transcribing the book—an error which faithful care on the part of subsequent transcribers has continued, because they have not dared to tamper with an inspired text. Whatever of difficulty exists in this single instance—and it is the most conspicuous and least explicable of any—it should not be allowed to throw any shadow over other parts of the Scriptures. Can there be any real shadow in the case of a man who is dying, and who is "filled with the Holy Ghost"? Certainly the trend of a divine inspiration is in Stephen. He is, if we must grant it, half oblivious to mathematical accuracy; but his great overmastering thought in his address is that some seventy or seventy-five souls have increased to an immense number, and out of them Christ has come; that Joseph's seed has produced Jesus; that the antetype has had its fulfillment in the "Holy and Just One," of whom the Jews "are the betrayers and murderers." His discourse is full of the trend of things. He sees the Holy Ghost as guiding events and men. He claims a divine ordering of events from first to last in the sketch of Hebrew history which he gives his auditors that day.

About these various readings it may well be claimed that we are not at the end of our difficulties, and claimed, just as fully, that in their study there are vast resulting confirmations.

Section III. Various Readings

In Westcott and Hort's introduction to "The New Testament in the Original Greek," Vol. II., pages 2 and 3, we read:

> With regard to the great bulk of the words of the New Testament, as of other ancient writings, there is no variation or other ground of doubt. The same may be said with substantial truth of those various readings which never have been received, and in all probability never will be received, into any printed text. The proportion of words virtually accepted on all hands is not less than seven-eighths of the whole. The remaining eighth, therefore, formed in great part by changes of order and comparative triviality, con-

stitutes the whole area of criticism. Setting aside difficulties in spelling, they make up one-sixtieth of the whole New Testament. Setting aside the comparatively trivial variations in this last estimate, the substantial variations can hardly be more than a thousandth part of the entire text. An exaggerated impression prevails as to the extent of possible textual corruption; and we desire to make it clearly understood how much of the New Testament stands in no need of a "textual critic's" labors.

Of course no inspiration is claimed for the very many transcribers who have undertaken to copy the original manuscripts, nor for those who copied from copies. No inspiration is claimed for printers of modern editions of the Bible. An instance of absolutely perfect printing in the case of so large a book as the Bible is unknown. Some error of spelling or punctuation, some mistake of word for word, or of letter for letter in numerals, is sure to be made. Even in the photographic processes of securing reprints of English books for American publishers, the slight angle of difference has obscured and obliterated some words. Those familiar with such subjects laugh at the alarm felt by others who have never examined this class of facts. Says President Hopkins: "By all the omissions and all the additions contained in all the manuscripts no fact is rendered obscure or doubtful." Says Bentley: "By none of these variations, etc., shall one be able to extinguish the light of a chapter or so disguise Christianity but that every feature of it will be the same." Says Maury: "In my investigations of natural phenomena when I can meet anything in the Bible it affords me a firm platform on which to stand."

INSPIRATION CONSIDERED AS A TREND

Section IV. Unintelligibleness

The unintelligibleness of the Bible is frequently alleged. It seems to be assumed that if the Bible is to make the truth clear, every part of it should be easily understood. But the question arises at once, "By whom should every part of it be understood?" Surely a man who comes to it with scanty knowledge of history, will not by opening the Bible at any place, become a fair judge about a historic allusion. Surely one may not demand that the Bible shall be so plain in every statement that no man shall ever make a mistake about it. That would be to demand a miracle in the case of every person of the race as he opens this book. How can a book that runs through the centuries, and is the production of men most subtile as philosophers, most imaginative as poets, most gifted as prophets, most logical as reasoners—how can such a book be intelligible, at the outset, to every reader? All things in it are not equally evident even to men of ordinary intelligence. Certain fundamental truths stand out clearly. Duty demanded by the claims of God is obvious, even to a child. He can see the way into the kingdom of God.

But the book is also for those beyond childhood, and beyond "ordinary intelligence." Progressive is the revelation in the book, and progressive is to be our understanding of it. Only in subsequent ages can much in the Bible become intelligible to the most earnest students and the most spiritual men. The book can only be fully understood when the history of the race on earth is completed and surveyed from the heights of glory. Many a man has texts laid by for the coming life; truths believed on abundant testimony, but only partially understood and awaiting the clearer light of the unveiled countenance of God. The book goes beyond this world. It is known now only in its beginnings. So that the mysteries are to a certain degree the proofs, and the gradual unveiling here indicates that it is a book that will bear the searching light of an eternity with God. Intelligible on some practical points, its very unintelligibility on others shows the inbreathing of God. The book of earth, it is the book of heaven. It foretells disclosures. The known makes us welcome the unknown, because the unknown is to be the known. Alike by what it reveals and by what it conceals we mark the inspiring trend.

A large number of prophecies in the Old Testament, especially of those relating to the coming of Christ, have not been fulfilled. Our Lord did not come in any such majesty as was there depicted. He was owned as Lord only by a very few persons and never by the Hebrew State. His dominion was not so extensive as therein declared. That he fulfilled some predictions is clear. And these predictions became actual history not only in their general spirit, but many of them were very minutely accomplished. The prophecies related to such matters as his bones, as when it was said, "Not a bone of him shall be broken"; to his dress, as when it was said of it, " Upon my vesture

**Section V.
Unfulfilled
Prophecy**

did they cast lots." It would sometimes seem as though the evangelists dwelt more on the great number of minute and verbal prophecies having a strictly literal fulfillment, than upon the general scope and tone of prophetic revelation, on which we to-day place so much stress. And this minuteness of prediction has been urged as strong objection to the biblical inspiration. The unfulfilled portions of these prophecies are so many that all of them have been called by an objector, " random predictions, some of which were sure of fulfillment, while others have completely failed."

But some of these prophecies are as broad as the whole future history of the world. They cannot yet be fulfilled. But those prophecies which have already become history are but the first-fruits and so are the earnest of those which await fulfillment.

We are living in a time when so much has been made of the alleged "prophecies," meaning thereby the strange guesses some have ventured on the obscure Book of Revelation, that there is a widespread reaction; and the exact and the literal fulfillment of Old Testament prophecy is liable to be received with some degree of discount. We are finding the whole Old Testament generally predictive rather than its separate verses especially prophetic. We are putting emphasis—not too much, but too exclusively—on the prophetic tone of every part of the older Scriptures.

But surely the directly prophetic words about the old cities of the Bible, relating as they do to the minutest things, are not to be set aside. The argument from fulfilled prophecy is to some minds the strongest proof they have of the inspiration of the Bible. Some men are so made as to look no further for evidence, when once they have seen the fulfillment of the very word of ancient prophecy.

God said, "I will utterly destroy the tongue of the Egyptian Sea." And Goshen once fruitful and beautiful has seen centuries of sterility, so that not a town or city was found upon it until the Suez canal was dug; and students of Egyptology have seen with amazement the exact and literal fulfillment of this prophecy. So too, the whole long series of prophecies about Noph, or Memphis, is distinguished for minuteness of detail. "Noph shall be without an inhabitant," said the prophet. It was a royal city, embracing a circuit of fifteen miles, the center of luxury, the pride of Egypt, But to-day not a human being resides in Noph. "Noph shall be desolate," said the prophet. Not a building stands in Noph. And while from their ruins the temples of Thebes, the other capital, can be restored on paper, any such restoration is impossible for Memphis. "Noph shall be laid waste," said the prophet again; tracing thus the successive stages of her overthrow. "You will walk," says another, "for miles through layers of bones and skulls and mummy swathings." Where once were fruitful gardens, the desert sands have invaded the soil and laid all waste. And yet, close by, the soil is grandly fertile in contrast with wasted Noph.

God said of Egypt as a whole, "I will lay her waste by the hands of strangers." There came speedily "the stranger." First, Nebuchadnezzar, with his Babylonians; then the Persians; then the Greeks; then the Romans. Then came the hordes of Constantinople; then the years of the Saracens; then the Mamelukes; then the Turks; then in modern days, the French; then the English "stranger," the whole land being virtually mortgaged to Great Britain to-day for the payment of the "Egyptian Bonds." And God said, "there shall be no more a prince from the land of Egypt." From a date older than authentic history, always a "prince"; from the time of the Persian conquest, never an Egyptian prince has ruled Egypt. But when the prophetic words were said the ruling dynasty of Egypt was the most ancient and stable on the earth.

There is the same startling minuteness in the special and peculiar predictions about Babylon. The successive steps of the sieges and the widely different methods to be employed by the conquerors of ancient Tyre are another marvel. The filling up of the strait between the island and the mainland, the failures at one point, the success at another during the final siege, are all predicted. So too, it is with those prophecies concerning Jerusalem as a city and Palestine as a land. They are almost microscopic in their detail. They read like history, though uttered in some cases centuries before the fulfillment. "What is the strongest proof of the Bible?" said Frederick the Great to a courtier. "Sire, the Jews," was the instant reply. There is a series of prophecies concerning Amalek, Nineveh, Babylon, Sidon, the Moabites, the Ammonites, the Philistines, the Chaldean monarchy, the Macedonian empire, and the Roman power. Often the things predicted are circumstances so unique as to be utterly beyond an uninspired ken. And the predictions about Christ, so varied, so peculiar, so minute and yet so broad, covering the scenes of his career from the manger to the ascension, are as far as possible from "fortunate guesses and general statements." The Gospel writers point out a very large number of these most unlikely fulfillments; and the intelligent reader finds additional instances constantly occurring to him as he peruses their glowing words.

But one of the most remarkable things about the gospel story is the presentation it gives us of Christ as the interpreter of prophecy. He was himself a prophet, but he is shown also as both endorser and interpreter of the Old Testament prophecies. Those who would find in prophecy only forecast, by the most general forms of language, of coming events, must stand rebuked before Christ's use of prophetic Scripture. He interprets it with a startling minuteness, not once or twice but continuously. Take the one subject of his resurrection. He refers to it frequently as a thing of prophecy. "Thus it is written" is his formula. He speaks of the slowness of heart in his disciples to believe "all that the prophets have written" on the theme of his resurrection. All this was "done according to the Scriptures," *i. e.*, the Old Testament. He was, he said, "the stone which the builders rejected," as foretold by the psalmist. These things are "written by the prophets concerning the Son." The Holy Ghost, by the prophets, had "testified beforehand the sufferings of Christ and the glory that should follow." Jesus said of himself, "the third day he shall rise again"; "Thus it is written and thus it behoved Christ to suffer and to rise from the dead the third day." The "thus it is written" is the prophecy in Hosea 6 : 2 : "After two day will he revive us; in the third day he will raise us up." There was a near fulfillment. But after that near fulfillment, our Lord quotes the words as a prophecy of his resurrection. Here it is not "general tone" nor "mere sound of similar words," but an actual prophecy concerning a circumstance that only the Holy Spirit could have foretold. Jesus uses the prophecy about "three days" so often that his enemies used it to point a sneer, when he was dead. They say, "We remember that while that deceiver was yet alive he said, After three days, I will rise again."

As with Christ's interpretation of prophecy, so it is with those given us by the apostles. In pointing out the fulfillment of minute prophecies they are especially earnest; and so they are our warrant in expecting direct and minute fulfillment of those that await accomplishment. Only let it be noted that these prophecies, the fulfillment of which was claimed by our Lord and his apostles, were not the vague statements of shrewd men venturing upon the possible contingencies in human affairs. The words are too definite, the predictions too careful, the details too many and unlikely, the circumstantial descriptions too exact for anything like that. God must have inspired these men to the extent of giving them a knowledge that no shrewdness or foresight could possibly furnish. Sometimes they did not themselves know all the meanings in their own predictions. They searched to find out what the inspiring Spirit really meant when it testified to a suffering Christ and the glory that should follow. In such cases God must have directed the word that carried in it reaches of divine thought greater than the writers knew. Other forms and degrees of care and superintendence might elsewhere suffice; but in the case of minute, far-reaching, and altogether unlikely prediction, a special inspiration must have been vouchsafed. And students of the facts which show the precise fulfillment of the most literal words of the prophetic books stand sometimes both delighted and amazed. They compare what God has wrought with what God has said. And they see in accomplished prophecy a nineteenth-century proof of the accuracy, credibility, and inspiration of the Scriptures.

These things being so, it cannot be said that those predictions not yet fulfilled are at all doubtful. The date is not yet ripe for some of them. "The fullness of time" is not yet come. God is not done with the world. The keystone is not yet set in the arch.

Then too, the methods of prophecy are not those of history. Prophecy does not see chronological but moral order as the prominent thing. It is not history written beforehand. Events are connected less in time and more in character. Things that are alike are massed. In the same passage there is reference to events centuries apart. A babe born in the prophet's day is connected, in prophetic vision and word, with a babe to be born hundreds of years afterward at Bethlehem. A prediction of the first coming carries, in a subordinate clause, a prediction of the second coming. A circumstance named in connection with a prophecy of the first advent is not fulfilled in the life of Jesus. It awaits his second advent. The two comings, utterly unlike in aim, as far apart as possible in their circumstances, are yet alike in this one thing, they are the comings of the Christ. The prophetic eye sees both and predicts both in a single sentence. This would be a false method in history, but it is a true method in prophecy. And the objection that has been raised on this account has simply shown a lack of knowledge of the real prophetic method. Let one get the point of view of the prophets, and the objections become confirmations.

But there are those who look less at single prophecies and more at the prophetic trend of the whole Old Testament. Both views are correct; nor does the specific invalidate the broader prophetic scope. It is equally unjust to slight either form of prophecy. There has been not a little unwise discussion whether the familiar phrase "in order that" means the exact fulfillment of specific words, or is only an illustration of an underlying principle announced originally by a prophet, but pointed out by an evangelist. The two may well be blended. The grammatical construction undoubtedly favors the former view. It looks, on the face of the Gospels, as if their writers so regarded it. They attach sometimes great force to a single word in a long prophecy. And yet they occasionally quote the principle rather than the specific word. Oftener however the two views are blended. It makes the prophecy less mechanical and the fulfillment less artificial, if we recognize the underlying principle. God is always prophesying in the Old Testament. The whole history of the mediating people is inspired. There are everywhere prophetic events, some very striking, some mainly of worth as showing the trend. There were constantly prophetic men; each exemplifying some one great virtue preparatory to the final advent of the Lord. So in the summer time you shall find an artist drawing here a tree, sketching there a mountain, giving now the course of some meadow brook, and then the outline of some lovely lake. He calls them "studies." He means by and by to assemble them all in the famous picture to be painted in the winter studio. So it is that in the Bible God gives us these prophetic events, prophetic men, prophetic rites, prophetic developments. They are studies toward the grand portraiture. The primal sin introduces the primal promise which gives token of the Calvary sorrow and the resulting salvation. The strange appearance of the priestly Melchizedek, without enrolled father or mother, who is not born and does not die on the pages of the record, is prophetic of the Christ who is the perpetual High Priest. So it is everywhere and with everything. Not an event is there that is not morally predictive. The exodus and the entrance, the captain appearing to Joshua, the strange episodes of the judges, the prosperous kingdom under Saul, David, and Solomon, the stormy days of political struggle with its humiliations and its salvations, the great captivity and the wonderful return—all of it is in the unmistakable trend, all of it is inspired history craving inspired record.

But the golden thread on which all the events are strung is that of Messianic prophecy. No other nation had such an inspiring thought as thrilled the Hebrews. One wonders that poetry, outside the Hebrew bards, did not dream of such a One. The king of a spiritual kingdom, the Christ anointed of God, the suffering Servant who is the appointed Saviour—all these are the various forms of the great idea that runs through the Old Testament. It is the union of a thousand separate threads woven into one firm fabric. All saviours from Israel's foes point to "the Saviour"; all salvation the "great Salvation"; all deliverers foretell "the Deliverer." A great thought is palpitating through the record and giving it its due form and its peculiar expression. The trend never turns aside. Steadily it grows in strength. It unifies all diversities. It is the great characteristic. It separates this literature to an immeasurable distance from all other national writings. All prophecies of every sort verge toward this Messianic fact. Not one of them is a deviation from this ultimate goal. The sunshine is stronger and stronger on the way in which all things run, and the prize at the end grows brighter as the centuries advance. Things are directed and the procession moves more swiftly; but the line of direction never alters. The bent knows no bending. There are eras of special revelation. The light gets stronger, now by steady increase and anon by sudden flashes. Sometimes the "word of the Lord was rare in those days"; sometimes there was "open vision." Always there was guidance. As in nature, so in revelation, there is variation, but God never loses his type. The divine thought is evermore reappearing. Dr. Harper has said:

> That Israelitish history is unique; that a nation was especially chosen by God from all the nations of the earth to do a work that should bless all the families of the earth; that Israel was especially guided in every step of national history; that disaster was the direct messenger of God; that prosperity was in the strictest sense the result of obedience to the divine command; that Jehovah, not a national deity, but the creator of all the earth, was his guide, his rock, his redeemer; that Israel's legislation was direct from heaven; that Israel's prophets spoke the exact word of God—all this the poets and prophets and sages declare repeatedly and emphatically. The events of Hebrew history stand alone. God acted in them as he acted in no others. Israelitish history is in a peculiar sense divine.—"*Biblical World,*" *Feb., 1895.*

History shows continually recurring divine laws. These are the constant principles out of which come the facts. So that by massing the facts we reason backward to the laws, and reason forward to the events. The Bible thus becomes one open book of eternal principles. It takes up facts wide centuries apart and puts them side by side. In his Epistle to the Galatians Paul names the two sons of Abraham as answering to Sinai and to Jerusalem. He says "Hagar is Sinai." "He who was of the bond-woman was born after the flesh; but he who was born after the free woman was born after the Spirit. Which things are an allegory." The attempt to put mystical meaning on such words has misled some good expositors. Once let the idea be clearly perceived that the great typical thoughts of "law and gospel," "nature and grace," are always present in the Old Testament history, and the "allegory" or instance, as Paul calls it, is simply the recurrence in other forms of the everywhere present thought that girds all parts of the Holy Scriptures into one compacted dominating aim and impulse and inspiration.

That the story of the Christian facts, even when reported by eye-witnesses, should be affected by the personal equation of the writer, is what we might expect. But what about the doctrinal teaching, the inner spiritual meaning of the facts? Do the doctrinal writers of the New Testament draw conclusions not only diverse but opposed to each other? If the logical deductions are not harmonious, is there not a blemish on the inspiration and would not this be an actual proof of non-inspiration?

Section VI. Discrepancy of View

The old conflict, so often alleged between Paul and James, is now relegated to the past. It is seen that Paul's doctrine of the justification of a sinner by faith is not inconsistent with the justification of a man's belief that he is a Christian as evidenced by his works. But so fierce was the contest over the alleged discrepancy that so good a man as Luther called James' epistle "an epistle of straw," and denied it to be an inspired writing. It was, indeed, only the passing vehemence of an earnest soul that had discerned one truth, and for the moment mistook his island for the whole broad continent. But the vigor of the language shows what was thought of the alleged discrepancy of view between James and Paul.

There has been developed of late a tendency to insist upon the difference between Paul and John. It would seem that some who dislike the doctrine would pit the apostle of justice against the apostle of love. There is a disposition to speak of Paul as forensically narrow and John as the disciple more nearly presenting the broad heart of his Lord.

There can be no doubt of the difference in the personality of the two men, and that this element comes out constantly in their epistles. Paul is a logician. He reasons. John never reasons, save with his heart. You can trace Paul's thought and find out why he says the next thing. John's connection of thought is simply a connection of feeling. Paul is doctrinal; John experimental. Paul is looking toward an end; John is the idealist who cares not for any related truth, nor where his idealism may lead him. Paul asks why a thing is done and how it is done; John seizes on the thing as done already. The idea of high solemn justice met and blended with compassion, and both manifested in Christ, dominates

Paul's thought, while the idea of God as light and love is regnant in the heart of John. Salvation is secured, in Paul's conception, through believing on Christ and so obtaining remission of sins and the witnessing Spirit. In John's idea, salvation comes from walking in the light and in fellowship with God, whose love is shown in giving Christ to be the propitiation for our sins. Men will always differ as to which is the root idea. Some will see the substantial unity of the two views.[1]

One asserts the atonement; the other assumes it. One has a certain systematic completeness; the other revels in the joyousness of truth, careless of all formal statement. We may not say that Paul was all brain and John all heart. For Paul's logic was often on fire with love, and John's love often sees clearly that we must be practical in our love to man as well as fervent in our love to God. The redeeming Christ, seen by the one on his cross, is seen by the other as the "Lamb of God" whose death is a "propitiation for the sins of the world." There is not a doctrine of Paul that has not an ample and direct recognition as a principle of life in John. And while the absolute artlessness of the latter contrasts strangely with

---

[1] This whole theme is thoroughly discussed in the able work of Dr. George B. Stevens, entitled "The Johannine Theology." The scope is so broad and the treatment so exhaustive that the book must remain a standard volume on this matter. The "Biblical World," March, 1894, contains an article by Dr. Stevens, giving an epitome of the views presented in the book above named, in which he shows that on the subjects of "The Idea of God," "The Person of Christ," "The Work of Christ," "The Doctrine of Sin," and the "Method of Salvation," there is no discrepancy between the two apostles.

the systematic form of Pauline statement, the trend is the same. The truth of life through Christ alone, of salvation by divine grace through a faith that issues in affectionate obedience, throbs through them both. The direction in which both move is the same and they are animated at every step by the same blessed Holy Spirit of God. The discrepancy is only of the surface. The inspiring trend is one. The forensic conception of salvation in Paul's epistles, the sacrificial conception in John, and the practical conception of the result of all the other conceptions as seen in James, are just so many different developments of the same great truth founded on the same great facts. The unity in the diversity shows the one ever-present trend of divine inspiration working through human facts, human hearts, and human words.

Section VII. Topographical Discrepancies

A few of these were alleged a quarter of a century ago. They arose from our imperfect knowledge of Egyptian and Babylonian history, chronology, and inscriptions. They are seldom mentioned to-day. But there is among those familiar with the mythology of the Greek and Roman writers a kind of suspicion. The older stories of the classic authors read in the college courses have made many persons not precisely distrustful, but at least willing to hear what can be said about the difference between Hebrew story and the Greek or Roman myth. Happily the better geographical and topographical researches of our time have done not a little to reassure any hesitating faith. For not only is there a vast multitude of agreeing and confirmatory testimony, as gathered by such men as Rawlinson [1] and others, showing the whole tone and coloring of the scriptural events to be in agreement with all we know of the alleged times and places where these events took place, but the whole mythological idea of the classic writers of the old Greek and Roman world is shown to sit so lightly on the hills and mountains, rivers and plains of the classic lands, that the myth can be disengaged and every scrap of history remain, while the Scripture events are part and parcel of Palestinian history and topography.

The landscapes of Greece would not be altered in the least by leaving out every line of Greek mythology. The supernatural could be blown off as a cloud from the surface of the earth, and every fact of history would be the same. Those legends were never attached save in the loosest and slenderest way to any locality. The Grecian myth had never an hour's serious belief even in the minds of those who used it in poetic license or in popular declamation. It was like our St. Nicholas and Santa Claus. It did well enough as the padding for polite literature among an imaginative people. They liked the beauty of the conception. It helped artist and singer and orator. It was never real to the people. It was a disembodied ghost. It had no time or place; no form, save in

---

[1] "Egypt and Babylon," by George Rawlinson.

fancy; no power, save as a pleasant fiction used to charm a weary hour. It never dreamed of affording proof from eye-witnesses. All was wrapped in mist. All was seen in haze. All was unreal, shadowy, evanescent. There was no locality, no basis of topography. No one said that these things must needs have been, Greece being what she was in her geographical position and her authentic history. You can lift off the legend, and the land is there. You can dissipate the mist, and that fair and famous old Athens is just the same.

But these gospel facts have historic and topographical anchorage. They occurred in the most critical age the world ever saw. Neither has geometry nor the science of evidence advanced a hair's breadth since that time. These facts occurred not in any obscure land, but in a country that fronted all three of the continents of the known world of that time, the most prominent and coveted portion of the earth. They occurred at Capernaum in the center of a dense population, and at Jerusalem, the chief literary city; also in the hill-country of Bethlehem and the upland towns of Galilee, all in the space of some forty miles, where men of extensive learning abounded and the Greek language and the Roman law prevailed. The supernatural of Palestine, exactly unlike that of Greece, is a veritable part of the history of the country itself. The facts are bound up with the land. The history and topography are blended in one common unity.

Says Professor Sayce, in the " Expository Times," December, 1891 :

There are numerous cases in which the discoveries of the last few years have re-established the credit of the Old Testament and dissipated the ingenious objections raised against them. Assyriology, Egyptology, prehistoic archæology, even explorations in southern Arabia and Asia Minor, have alike been contributing to this result. . . The second half of the fourteenth chapter of Genesis, that which recounts the meeting between Abram and Melchizedek, has also received a remarkable confirmation from the clay records of the past. It is from the tablets of Tel el-Amarna that the light in this instance has been derived. The confirmation thus unexpectedly afforded of the historical trustworthiness of the two narratives in the fourteenth chapter of Genesis opens up a still larger question. It shows that underneath the narratives of Genesis lie historical documents which come down from the age of the events which they record, and possess accordingly all the value of contemporaneous evidence. Whatever may have been the period when the book was compiled, its author or authors made use of written materials, and these written materials were as historically trustworthy as those on which we base our knowledge of the Persian wars with Greece. The history of Canaan before the Israelitish conquest was not a blank to be filled up by the legends and systematizing fictions of a later day. It belongs to a period when reading and writing were widely known and practised, and when contemporaneous events were recorded in imperishable clay.

Rawlinson, quoting the story of Abraham's visit to Egypt as recorded in Genesis 12 : 10–20, calls attention to particular after particular therein enumerated, and shows how each was matched in "secular history." Egypt is a monarchy. Egypt has princes under a monarchy with specific duties; the names of the monarch, Pharaoh, "the Great House," and those of officers, who are to report the coming of any body of foreigners into the kingdom, being given. In one division of Egypt forage abounds. Domesticated animals named in the story in Genesis are exactly those found at that time in Egypt; but the horse is apparently in that age unknown. These notices of the Scripture clearly show the sort of civilization then existing in that land. Rawlinson also quotes Gen. 39 : 2–20; and then shows "that this picture is in remarkable harmony with the general tone of Egyptian manners and customs." A large number of these special instances of this harmony are given by him. It is the same with Joseph's time; customs then named having been unknown in Abraham's day. Precisely the same thing has been shown by Rawlinson in his "Notices of Egypt in Exodus and Numbers"; also in Kings and the earlier prophetic writing. Each book has its setting in the customs of its own time, in contemporary manners and in historic facts.

These books are not historic novelettes, for "the spade" has shown the proofs of historicity. Light came in as to these contemporary facts and historic confirmations, first, from the annals of Sargon, by which we have the record of expeditions of Babylonian kings who had lived and reigned long before the time of Abraham. Sayce insists that "for the archæologist, the Pentateuch is rooted in the Mosaic age." Conder, of the Exploration Fund, tells us that "things that could not be said three years ago can be said now about the ancient civilizations and their remarkable agreement, topographically, with the Bible story." We have learned that the old cultures of Egypt, of Assyria, and even of the

Palestinian peoples, were vastly in advance of what had been believed; that the old world of Abraham and Jacob and Joseph and Moses was a world of books and libraries; that men were capable of recording historic facts with accuracy; that kings employed scribes to do this thing; that there was even international correspondence in clay letters between the people on the banks of the Euphrates, the Jordan, and the Nile. It has been claimed that historic material as worthy of credence was furnished three thousand years ago as that given us within the last three hundred years for what we call modern history.[1]

If a stable government, organized institutions, developed art and papyri preserved in ancient tombs, now as legible as when first written four thousand—some claim five thousand—years ago; if tablets of clay hardened into imperishable stone can furnish a basis of historic facts; and if the historic faculty existed, as shown by the oldest Egyptian book—and all this has been proved—then we have the opportunity newly furnished to our age for comparing sacred and secular history in their tone and spirit, in their recorded customs and their whole mode of thought, feeling, and action. And the correspondences are multiplying. The few minor discrepancies—one hardly knows how to state them, they are so few—vanish before the ac-

---

[1] "That the art of writing, and with it historical and other literature, came with the earliest Egyptian colonists there seems no reason to doubt. The oldest monuments show it in as great perfection as at any subsequent date." Dawson, "Egypt and Sinai," pp. 159, 160.

cumulated light of unintentional agreements and correspondences. The book is of God, as well as of man. It is everywhere dominated by a trend that is historical as well as religious. One thought from one Mind rules it from first to last.

The alleged savagery of the Old Testament has been repeatedly urged as a blot upon an inspired book. About this sanguinary element some things are to be said frankly. It is (1) apparent in the record, and we find it sometimes in the sayings of good men. One meets conspicuous instances of it in the Psalms. So too, (2) this vindictiveness in the story comes sometimes from the fact that these bloody wars were religious wars waged against the Jehovah religion for its exclusive character. Good men had to be slaughtered or to resist by force of arms. Whatever may have been said later in New Testament times, no idea of nonresistance was found in the Old Testament, when Israel was attacked by her foes. So too, (3) these conspicuous facts of vindictiveness should have been accurately recorded if they actually existed. Nor is the Bible in its record of these wars any more to blame than is secular history for its record of other wars. And further, (4) the vindictiveness is often a form of intense opposition to the wrong. Some psalms can only be fitly read in war times. They have a different tone in such periods of national indignation at unrighteousness. There were hours during our late Civil War when men turned to these most terrible war cries, nor found

Section VIII.
Alleged Savagery

them too strong to voice their moral wrath at the enemies of righteousness. But (5) there is a reason deeper than any other. David is usually reckoned as a chief offender. And there is a wide—an immensely wide chasm between the morality of the man and the religion of the man. Let us own this frankly. We are really amazed to find this man of tenderest soul, who in his most devotional moods is leading the songs of the ages, so sadly wrong in conduct and so vindictive in spirit. Men who are opposed to the book say, "Well, here is your 'man after God's own heart,' and he is religious enough toward God, but he is wicked enough toward men." These are the facts—a very spiritual man, as shown in his holy songs, and a wicked man at times, as shown in his conduct. We do well to make some abatement by showing that his wickedness was succeeded by a "return to God." But we shall find it hard to be severe upon him when we see him moaning and sobbing out his penitence before God in his fifty-first Psalm. One must be hard-hearted and of bitter and vindictive judgment himself, who can see him on his knees in confession and not consider this fact of his great penitence.

But all this extenuation may be admitted and still there is left a sad record of vindictive deeds. Now let there be seen on the pages of sacred story the whole broad series of facts. God did select this man when he was plainly very imperfect. He did not take him as a man advanced in morality or practical holiness. He was a backward saint, at first, even by a low standard. In his best days he was not a specially advanced man in the humanities. And yet he is especially forward in religion. Plainly then he is more than himself in his songs. He speaks for another and by that other's help. Only as we assume a direct, express, peculiar inspiration of God's Holy Spirit, very far in advance of his personal character, can we understand him or his work. He is more than the weak man David. He has, indeed, natural poetic gifts. But he himself and his muse are taken up of God. His inspiration is not measured by his religion. His own backwardness stands right over against his wonderful forwardness in spiritual song. He is inspired of God above the measure of his own moral, religious, and spiritual attainments. He is moved upon, in his song by a peculiar influence, raising him, in some respects, above himself. He sings as it were impossible he should sing otherwise than as influenced by the Holy Spirit. His inspiration is more than himself. This is the only explanation of David. He is proof and instance of what God can do in this direction for men who in their character are sadly fallible, when he will take and use them. They have what we must call a peculiar inspiration directly from God. And the man when thus moved, comes into the trend. He sings often New Testament songs before their time. He is more than David the man; he is David the divinely inspired seer, the prophet of the Lord. It was a case of the fulfillment, before they were uttered, of Christ's words, "It shall not be ye that speak." In this case inspiration is explanation.

Section IX. Continuous Revelation

Arguing on the theory that inspiration is simply a form of personal religious utterance, and so is measured by each man's personal piety, some have asked why the trend may not be continuous, and men be as much inspired now as in former times. In his "Yale Lectures," Mr. R. F. Horton adopts this view, representing the preacher as receiving his message directly from God, exactly as did the ancient prophets. He claims "a revelation that *is* as well as a revelation that *was*." On this ground revelation, in the sense of a continued Bible made up of experiences and revelations for the last nineteen hundred years, is to be consulted as is our Bible. So Schleiermacher is understood, in some of his utterances, to put no emphasis on biblical inspiration as a thing different from that which comes from the utterance of any Christian soul, in the speaking of the truth that may be perceived.

There can be an instant "test of fact" in replying to such a statement. Are the religious teachers of to-day comparable with the New Testament writers in divine inspiration? Take the foremost books that have influenced men for the last two centuries. The most widely known religious book of the former century was Bunyan's "Pilgrim's Progress"; the most widely read religious volumes of the last quarter of a century are "Spurgeon's Sermons." Try these books by Mr. Horton's standard. Have they the same authoritativeness in tone? Have they the evidence anywhere of the same inspiration as that of Paul and John?

How the authors of these modern books would have shrunk in holy horror from such a claim. They held the Bible to be inspired in a sense they never dared claim for their own productions. They did hold that the Holy Spirit illuminated their minds to see, feel, interpret, and present anew the truth found in the inspired word—a very different thing.

So too, there is the test of the readers as well as of the writers. Do Christians feel that they are presented with the direct speech of God in these last-named books, as they do when they open their Bibles? Surely "the test of Christian consciousness," to which such men as Mr. Horton and Mr. F. W. Robertson and those who intimate a "universal divine inspiration among Christians" are wont to appeal so strongly, is against their view in this matter.

No more is the claim exemplified in those who make it. It is not seen that they are more spiritual as men, nor more divinely persuasive as teachers. They are not more conspicuously "filled with the Holy Ghost" than their brethren in the ministry. They always, when they come to the personal appeal, fail to put in this claim for themselves. They shrink with all due modesty, as David and Isaiah and Paul and John did not. But the inspired prophets never shrank, never hesitated. They boldly laid claim to direct divine inspiration. That the "Yale Lectures" do not show the same evidence of divine inspiration as do the Pastoral Epistles, is no reflection upon the Lectures. They are another kind of production, having many excellencies and much to commend them; but they belong in another realm of literature. They show the logical unsoundness of the main position they set themselves to defend. Bound up together with the Bible in the same volume, by sheer force of the bookmaker's art, there might be a demand for one edition, but no second edition would be printed. The testing in any way, of the position, shows its erroneousness. Let exposition of the sacred word be claimed for such human productions; let them be regarded as contributions to a better understanding of human duty. But who does not shrink from calling them God's word?

Further; not only do our human productions on religious themes fail to come up to the level of God's word, but they often differ from it. In that case, according to the theory of a continuous divine inspiration, which of them shall stand as the true word of God for us? Coming later, derived from a purer piety, a larger knowledge, a higher tone of Christian morality than was possible to Christians in the apostolic age, the newer revelation will be the better of the two. The "modern Christian consciousness" considered as a Bible, will rightly supersede the former Bible. In that case we ought to read into it our newer, better convictions of what it should say, and of what it would say had it been written in our own century. Somebody once rewrote "Pilgrim's Progress," one of the most spiritual of books, in the interest of ritualism. And the moral scorn of the Christian world was only equaled by the literary scorn of foremost reviewers. To re-write the Bible in the interests of the theory of a "continuous inspiration like in kind to that of the biblical writers," would be a necessary but a terrible duty, from which none would shrink more heartily than some who have not duly considered the trend of their mistaken position.

There is no antecedent reason why the Old Testament should not stop at a given point, and none why the New Testament should not have a close. One might not beforehand say where a period should be put to either volume. But now that it has been done, we can mark the wisdom that began and ended the Bible. It is with revelation as it is in nature with the creation of man, the end everywhere typified is reached. Says Winchell: "The column of organic succession is complete in man. The lower forms, gradually and regularly ascending from base to summit, constitute the shaft of the column; but in man we have a sudden expansion, an ornateness of finish, an incorporation of new ideas which designate him as the capital and completion of the grand column of organic existence. No further progress can be made in this direction." There is the fulfilling of all former predictions of nature in man, the creature; and similarly all prophecies of inspiration are fulfilled in the New Testament. It expects to be superseded by no other book.

Careful study and reflection on the scope of the revelation God has given us show the rounded

---

[1] "Sketches of Creation," p. 377.

completion of the work undertaken. We praise God for what he has given. We might ask, in our merely curious moods, for more. Sometimes we long, in the progress of the undertaking, for a few words here and there to help us understand the Bible more completely. But our more sober thought is as glad over the silences as it is over the utterances of the Scriptures. The trend finds consummation. It brought us on to Christ; then on to his church as founded and directed by apostolic teaching. The apostles could have no successors. Verbal testimony as to a risen Christ by men appointed of God who saw him after his resurrection, must end with their death. But this ripe, rounded New Testament, they have left behind for us, claiming for it the fulfillment of their Master's promise, "He," *i. e.*, the Holy Spirit, "shall lead you into all truth." These men followed out in their verbal and in their written story this promised leading, this divine trend; and it is ours to mark this trend everywhere visible in their thought and deed and word.

INDEX

Adam, created in righteousness and holiness, 102.
Abraham: and coming Christ, 88; attempted offering of Isaac, 108.
Age-spirit, danger from, 59.
Alleged facts, either true or immoral, 23.
Alleged errancy, 179.
Antagonisms in argument to be avoided, 35.
Anthropomorphism, 166, 206.
Apostolic representations, 202.
Approximations in all theories, 35.
Apprehend, to, not to comprehend, 40.
Apostles not mentally or morally superior, 203.
Assumptions: necessary in mathematics, 19; of outside world, 49; of inspiration of Bible by good men, 136.
Argument for Divine existence and Divine inspiration similar. Introduction.
Assyrian ante-Mosaic belief, 101.
Athenian fancies, 235.
Authorship: not always avowed, 154; often assumed as known, 155.
Authentic documents needed, 28.
Autobiography of Moses, 83.
Axioms: in mathematics, 25; in logic, 46; in morals, 47.

Balfour, quotation from, 138.
Basis: in New Testament, 45; in Old Testament, 46; in intuitions, 47.
Belief: in self, 48; in substance other than our bodies, 48; in other minds, 49; in the true and the false, 50; postures experiential, 118.
Bengel, quotation from, 103.
Bently, quotation from, 217.
Bible: hold of on middle classes, 14, 28; a growth, 72; bound to account for, 16; awakes moral convictions, 70; universal utterances of, 75; wide plan of, 139; completion of, 245; no one class addressed in, 14; of great value, 71; a human book, 175.
Biography as a method of history, 82.
Bruce, quotation from, 44, 60.

Caiaphas, prophecy of, 197.
Canonical books, 143.
Capacity for being inspired, 117.
Christ: endorsement of Old Testament by, 163; his interpretation of prophecies, 223; his interpretation of the facts of the Old Testament in the New Dispensation, 110.
Christian consciousness: argument from, 123, 135; agreement of, with written word, 131.
Christianity: exists, 45; connected with a book, 47.
Chronological difficulties: recog

247

nized, 208; exist in other ancient books, 209.
Coleridge's view of Old Testament, 96.
Contemporary Review, quotation from, 57.
Conant, quotation from, 106.
Contents of Christian consciousness, 115.
Continuous inspiration, 133, 242.
Co-partnership of Bible and human intuitions, 175.
Co-relation of fact and record, 174.
Cross references of biblical writers, 159.

Davis, quotation from, 164.
David's piety not the measure of his inspiration, 241.
Daniel's prophetic mood, 196.
Danger of technical studies, 49, 129.
Dawson, quotation from, 238.
Deborah's song, 170.
Deliverances and the Deliverer, 171.
Development of conception, 106
Devotional use of Bible, 134.
Difficulties in discarding the Bible, 17.
Difficulties may be confirmations, 206.
Divine guidance in common events, 192.
Dormant intuitions, 60.
Dynamic theory, 32.

Elements of truth in each theory, 33.
Egyptian beliefs, 101.
Enoch's prophecies, 103.
Erasmus, quotation from, 136.
Events: cumulative, 76; inspired record of, 33.
Evidence, human certainty by, 180.

Existence, the Divine. Introduction.
Experimental religion: as to the Bible, 126; its methods of proof, 123; its limitations, 124; its certainties, 126; its corrections, 133; its echo of biblical fact and doctrine, 135.
Eye, the vital, 34.
Ezekiel's prophecies, 169.

Fairbairn, quotation from, 117, 132.
Farrar, quotation from, 87.
Feeling, a fact to be recognized, 125.
Flowers concentrated sunshine, 114.
Final authority in religion, 141.
Force, vital, 15.
Future life: in historical books, 103; in Pentateuch, 104; in prophets, 105.

Garbett, quotation from, 199.
Geographical exactness and inexactness, 78.
Genius: human, in Bible, 32; in plan of books, 96.
God: argument for existence of. Introduction. Argument for, of trend, 39; necessitarian view of, 37; teleological view of, 38; as a logical being, 62; as a moral being, 63; arguments for, same as for inspiration, 40.

Hackett, quotation from, 215.
Hamilton, quotation from, 62.
Harper, quotation from, 88, 114, 229.
Hebrew race: foremost morally, 21; historic existence of, 45.
Hegelianism, 23.
Historians: best are biographers, 82; necessarily prophetic,

though humanly so, 95; Mosaic method revived by, 97.
Hitchcock, quotation from, 91.
Holy Spirit: interpreter, 109; inspirer, 150.
Homeric methods of description, 81.
Homiletic use of Bible, 135.
Horton, quotation from, 131.
Hopkins, quotation from, 217.

Importance of inquiry, 13, 20.
Increasing knowledge, 185.
Induction as a method: defined, 42; limitations of, 43; deduction not wholly separated from, 42; only probable conclusions reached by, 44.
Influence of Bible, 14.
Inerrancy, 182.
Inspiration: burden of proof on opponents, described rather than defined, 29; of facts, 190; thrones of, 32; human, 34; endorsement of, by other inspired men, 157; various ways of considering. Introduction; verbal, 32.
Interpretation (full) of Old Testament only in New, 99.
Intuition: corroborated by reason, 56; trustworthy, 58.
Investigators should be experimental Christians, 135.

Judaism: exists, 45; connected with a book, 46.
Judean topography, 236.
Judgment day: intuitive belief in, 54; also reasonable, 55.

Kilpatrick, quotation from, 210.
Kidd, quotation from in "Social Evolution," 58.
Knowledge, human, not unreliable, 44.

Libraries, ancient, on stone and papyrus, 238.
Life, to be described not defined, 17.
Life and immortality brought to light, 160.
Literalness of biblical events, 100.
Literary imperfection not moral error, 74.
Literature (human) the expected form of revelation, 151.
Livingstone, quotation from, 57.
Luther's view of James' Epistle, 231.

Maury, quotation from, 217.
Material, literary, in Palestine, 162.
Maurice, quotation from, 23.
Max Müller, quotation from, 50.
Measure of piety not that of inspiration, 186, 203.
Men free though inspired, 151.
Methods: those to be used, 29; historical, 79; optical, 80.
Mill: quotation from, on consciousness, 47; on induction, 115.
Miracle: not a buttress, but truth incarnate, 194; demand for, 75;
Moral intuitions, 48–54.
Morrison, quotation from, 58.
Moses: method of in writing, 81; code of, 97; in wilderness, 34.
Monotheistic idea always preserved, 169.
Multiplication table, 19.
Mutual consistency of intuitions, 62.
Myer on Egyptian Archæology, 52.

Names of scriptural writings, 203.
Natural intuitions, 42.
Noah's work, 103.
Norms: in ten commandments, 119; in regeneration as a condi-

tion of admission to kingdom, 121.
Old nations monotheistic, 50.
Old Testament interpreted by New, 93.
Oral preaching by apostles, 142, 203.
Owen, George, quotation from, 57.

Paul: Epistles of, 200; his exceptions, 201.
Pentateuchal history, 96.
Perplexities, greater without inspiration, 24.
Plain men best witnesses, 18.
Poetic quotations in Psalms, 171.
Prayer to know the truth, 16.
Premonitions of New Testament in Old, 101.
Preservation of Bible, 186.
Proctor's description of optical phenomena, 91.
Post-exilic theory of Pentateuch, 163.
Prophecies: of Noph, 220; of Memphis, 221; of Babylon, 222; of Tyre and Jerusalem, 223.
Prophecy not history, 225.
Prophets did not know all the meanings of their words, 224.
Progress in doctrine, 168.
Promises carry with them facts, 121.
Primitive beliefs: gone back to, 46; trustworthy when reached, 66.

Rawlinson, quotation from, 56.
Reading the New Testament with the Old, 113.
Record of events unique, 89.
Relation of the Old to New, 91.
Rejection of inspiration, 26.
Renan: remarks of, 58; his mistake, 162.

Redemption: a fundamental idea of the world, 89; of single souls, 90.
Resurrection in Old Testament, 105.
Results, 21.
Responsibility for reception or rejection, 16.
Revelation: the, 7; John's method in, 81.
Robertson, quotation from, 172.
Robinson, quotation from, 215.

Sanguinary Psalms, 239.
Sanity of biblical writers, 184.
Sayce, quotation from, 235.
Scenes, of facts and persons, 23.
Schleiermacher, quotation from, 87.
Scriptures affectionately regarded, 144.
Search simplified by inspiration, 25.
Secular versus religious scholarship, 197.
Self-knowledge not easy, 65.
Semitic carelessness about dates, 209.
Shairp, quotation from, 80.
Smith, quotation from, 189.
Stevens, quotation from, 232.
Spiritual instincts, 16, 37.
Spurgeon, quotations from, 183.
Subjects that demand inspired record, 143.
Symbols, in their New Testament interpretation, 112.

Testimony of experience, 124.
Theory, none absolutely consistent, 84.
Theories: in their agreement, 30; parallel, 35; each theory explains some things, 32; dynamic theory, 31; verbal theory, 33;

INDEX

thought theory, 32; all to be recognized, 35; no one held consistently, 31.
Trend: definition of, 29, 32; covers all theories, 33; traced everywhere, 198, 199; in argument for God, 38; of the book, 31; of each view, 30; magnetic, 29; strength of, 246.
Universal expectation of inspiration, 141.
Uninspired Bible would hurt us rather than help, 21.
Verification: of fact by experience, 127; of one method by another, 129.
Vital eye, 34.

Warranted expectations, 152.
Whateley's definition of induction, 42.
Wordsworth's poetical descriptions scientific, 80.
Worth of experience in argument for others, 123.
Winchell, quotation from, 245.
Wrong conception of Bible: is vital wrong against self, 17; is against God, 18.

www.ingramcontent.com/pod-product-compliance
Lightning Source LLC
Chambersburg PA
CBHW032109220426
43664CB00008B/1195